The Colour *of the* Sun

The Colour *of the* Sun

a memoir

Gillian Thorp

E. L. Marker
Salt Lake City

E. L. Marker, an imprint of WiDō Publishing
Salt Lake City, Utah
widopublishing.com

Events in this book may be slightly out of sequence and some names have been changed to protect the privacy of individuals. Otherwise, it is a completely true story told from my perspective growing up. I have made every effort to ensure that events, locales, and conversations from my memories are as accurate as possible.

Cover design by WildEagles
Book design by Marny K. Parkin
Sun image from frepik.com

ISBN 978-1-947966-40-6

Contents

South Africa

The House on Barnes Road   9

iFafa   53

Greenwood Park   73

America

Ventura, California   119

Reno, Nevada   135

The East Coast   193

Santa Clara, California   213

Dedication and Acknowledgments   247

About the Author   249

SOUTH AFRICA

"So many went on a quest to tame her,
The only man to win her heart was the one
Who was also free." —Nikki Rowe

The House on Barnes Road

1

I WAS BORN AMONG THIEVES.

What was stolen from me will not seem valuable to you, I am sure, and yet this theft quite possibly defined the trajectory of my life. If you believe in such things—which I'm still not sure I do.

You see, on that June afternoon in Durban, South Africa, when my mother pushed me out into the harsh hospital light, I was shrouded in a caul. This type of birth, when a baby emerges inside the amniotic sac, or caul, is one of the rarest in the world. Over the millennia, many cultures came to consider the caul to be mystical, and babies born inside one special, destined for good fortune and perhaps even possessing supernatural powers.

South Africa of 1971 was one of those cultures, and my family recounted many times how the doctors and nurses marveled over me.

Hours after my birth, my caul was stolen. Perhaps it was stolen by sailors, who were known to bribe midwives for a baby's caul, believing they prevented drowning. Or perhaps, as Aunty Val suggested, it was the bloody nurses. "*Ja,* no doubt," Mummy agreed. "Those bladdy nurses would sell a child for a Krugerrand." Either way, the mystical shroud that had promised me good fortune, and marked me as special, was gone.

If I were inclined to believe in ancient superstitions—and how can one ever be certain either way?—then the person who took my veil also bore my good fortune away with them in the dark.

What is certain is that fortune did not follow me home from the hospital.

I would have told you otherwise during my youngest years. I thought my family and I were very fortunate. The greatest proof of this was right before my eyes, vibrant red and smooth to the touch: our very own car.

A car was a great luxury for a family of Coloureds, as people of mixed European and African or Asian heritage were known in South Africa at the time. Most Coloured men and women relied on public transportation to get to and from work and run everyday errands, but my family—we drove. We didn't have to wait at bus stations in the rain or walk long miles carrying young children or groceries in Durban's tropical heat. My father carefully drove each of us three kids and my mother home from the hospital in that car, and later, as we grew, he took my siblings and me for countless rides. He took us to visit relatives, and he shuttled elderly neighbors to and from the grocery store. The Fiat did everything asked of it; it was a marvel, a convenience launching us into a different realm of existence. And yet, in hindsight, I wish he had never bought it.

To fully grasp what happened in the decades later, you must understand the man from whom it all sprang. The man who set in motion all that was to come for my family with a single, irrevocable choice.

Let's say, by some miracle, you could view the Earth from two hundred miles above the African continent during the summer of 1968. Look around you, and you will see storm fronts, the white of the poles, patches of clear skies, vast seas, and the fractionalized outlines of continents.

Your eye settles on the east coast of Africa and traces a path along the coastline 2,065 miles south of the equator where it falls on Durban: a city of some three-quarters of a million people, the busiest seaport in the country of South Africa. You see container ships and oil tankers slowing to enter the harbor and accelerating to leave it, barely avoiding each other, not to mention whatever— or whomever—else might have exercised questionable judgment in crossing the busy bay, either by choice or necessity.

Let's say your eyes continue to explore. They fall upon a busy metropolitan area, punctuated with buildings reaching toward the sky, surrounded by neighborhoods where a teeming assortment of smells clamors for the attention of your nose: Durban curry being cooked in homes; *boerewors* sausages roasting on fires' smoke from outdoor *braais*; spices wafting from the open crates at Indian stores darkened by the shadow of Apartheid, a shadow you almost miss from so high above, but as you look closer, you see signs that read COLOUREDS ONLY and BLANKE GEBIED. Close your eyes, take a deep breath and enjoy the smells of the abundant flora: mango trees, wild bananas, and the sprawling, ground-creeping Hottentot fig; tea leaves growing on plantations; burnt sugar from the mills built to process the bounty of the sugarcane fields along the coastal belt where the Umgeni and Msunduzi Rivers spill into the Indian Ocean.

This brings your attention back to the Bay of Durban, and your gaze drifts toward the rolling waves south of the harbor. Let's say, too, it's a weekend, and you see a figure knifing through the waves and troughs, challenging the African sea. The figure, upon even more minute inspection, is a young man in his twenties, hair slick with water, bare feet sturdily planted on a surfboard, his thin, muscular body twisting toward the sea, the sky, the shore. He is surfing on the Coloured side of Durban's Indian Ocean, where the beaches and breaks are less desirable—his fair skin perhaps raising eyebrows. That man is my father, and he is smiling big enough for you to see.

Born out of wedlock, Edgar Victor August would never know his father. His mother, an exceptionally private and reserved Coloured woman, had been one of twelve children and was just as much a puzzle as my father was. Fair-skinned, with a round nose and sad green eyes, I don't ever recall hearing her laugh. Granny August, as we called her, had a relationship with a white European soldier stationed in the mining town of Kimberly during WWII, and the result of their union was my father. Before learning of her pregnancy, the soldier was transferred out of South Africa. He would never know of the birth of his son, nor see again the young Coloured woman he had once impressed. Only a few years later, such relationships would become criminalized.

Coloured people came about as a result of colonial settlers arriving during the seventeenth century and engaging in relations with African locals. Generations later, the Coloured community became an ethnic group, like many other groupings within South Africa's borders, and in 1948, we became subject to our own unique limitations under Apartheid.

Apartheid, to put it in as frank terms as possible, was a nonsensical system that highlighted the dark side of mankind. Race was sometimes determined by laughable tests—though there was nothing humorous about them, as families were known to be separated depending on the results. There was the pencil test, for example, where a pen or pencil was put into your hair, and you were then instructed to shake your head. If the pencil remained stuck, this would indicate kinkiness, meaning you were non-White. But such tests were usually not tests of exoneration but rather affirmation. If you failed, it was simply confirmation you were Coloured, but if you "passed," well, mostly, you remained Coloured. If you were Chinese or Japanese though, no test was necessary: Chinese were automatically considered Coloured, and Japanese were honorary Whites.

Irrationally absurd? Yes, I would say so.

Despite the country boasting a thoroughly modern infrastructure, resources for hospitals and mental health facilities were funneled toward the White population (or Europeans, as they were also called). Being White under the forced segregation of Apartheid meant you received the best services and options available—healthcare, education, employment, housing, and so on—while non-Whites (Africans, Indians, Asians, and Coloureds) were forced to live in separate and less desirable areas with limited resources and opportunities. Starting in 1948, the South African government (all Whites of English and Dutch descent) set up a framework of legal boundaries to enforce physical segregation between the racial groups in a way that affected virtually every aspect of life.

People often speak of Apartheid in terms of its categorization and compartmentalization of people by colour. But my father, with his skin as white as the keys on a grand piano, dark blond hair, and ocean-blue eyes, had colouring identical to heavyweight boxer Daan Bekker who would represent White South Africa in the 1960 Olympics. Yes, South Africa cared about colour, but it was blood that drew the lines which separated Black from White. This left a lot of grey, so to speak, and that grey resided primarily in the Coloured communities.

My father and mother met at the Himalaya.

Located in Durban's Coloured area, the Himalaya was the setting for wild nights of dancing each weekend. Mummy recalls it as being a real *jol*. Coloured and Indian audiences would shed the inhibitions that shrouded them during the weekdays, moving freely to local entertainment from Durban's popular music scene—Dukes Combo, The Flames and Erol Shultz—punctuated with the rich aroma of Indian curry and rice, bunny chows and chili bites as the afternoon turned to evening, then night. On the second floor of the Himalaya, my mother danced the *langarm,* and this is where my father first saw my mother. She had smooth brown skin, long black hair, and a chin, which narrowed to a defined and dainty V. Her nose was narrow and pointed, her eyebrows plucked into thin black lines. My father approached this woman and asked her to dance. At 6′5″, he stood taller than most men, and I'm sure there were many that night who wondered what a White person was doing at the Himalaya. Mummy told me she had initially refused him until he assured her that despite his appearance, he was, in fact, Coloured. The distinction might seem absurd, but it was only by virtue of that nuance my mother was able to accept his offer, and their journey together could begin.

How they fell in love is its own story, but in order to continue with this story, you must know they did.

After sharing a long walk and conversation where they planned their new life together, my mother and father found themselves on a park bench in town, bodies pressed close together, hands clasped.

A voice interrupted them, "Hey! You two," and they looked up to see a police officer standing over them. "What do you think you're doing?"

"I'm sorry," my father said, "but I don't see a problem here, officer."

"I don't have time for bladdy games. You both know it's illegal for the two of you to be together."

"But we're both Coloureds," my father said.

"Look here, stop with the games, or I'm going to throw her in bladdy jail."

Father insisted, "Really, there are no games here. I'm not white."

"Where do you live?"

"In town, on Center Street."

"Okay, let's go. I need to verify this."

When my mother told me this story as a child, I remember laughing, imagining the officer's embarrassment when it was verified that my father was not White. Now that I'm older and decades removed from that time and place, I cannot laugh at this story. Think of it: this police officer saw what he thought was a White man canoodling with a Coloured woman in a Coloured neighborhood. Under Apartheid, this was illegal. And yet, it was the Coloured woman in her own neighborhood who was threatened with jail. Under Apartheid, Whites were never wrong.

FATHER CONSTANTLY HAS TO ASSURE OTHERS HE IS Coloured.

Mummy and Father have been courting for a while. He is walking toward her parents' house in the Coloured neighborhood of Sydenham when a group of Coloured men intercept him.

"Hey, *ek se!* What's a honky like you doing here in Sydenham?"

Father tries to assure them he is a *Bruin Ou* and will soon be marrying David Tucker's daughter. He pulls a white slip of paper from his trouser pocket, my mother's address written in dark ink in his careful hand. He shows it to the men threatening him with knives, accusing him of crossing Apartheid boundaries. "You know David Tucker, right?" he says. "He's going to be my father-in-law."

But the men, segregated for the colour of their skin by laws which regard only blood, say, "You bladdy *Wit Ou,* we'll show you a thing or two, coming round here." And they chase him through the streets of Sydenham until my father, sweating, full of adrenaline, finally escapes on a bus. He knows he will have to once again prove his race, and he feels the injustice of this deeply, but his love for my mother eclipses his anger. Besides, by now, he has grown used to it.

It takes a meeting, arranged by David Tucker, my future grandfather, to convince the neighborhood boys that while my father looks like a *Wit Ou,* his blood is as brown as theirs.

"Look here," my grandfather says, showing them a copy of my father's birth certificate, "the man is Cape Malay." My father, Edgar, as everyone in the neighborhood will call him, is Cape Malay, a subcategory of the Coloured group, and so they accept him, and a plot of rich African dirt in a Coloured neighborhood of Durban gives way to a house for my mother, aged twenty, and my father, twenty-five.

I DON'T KNOW PRECISELY WHEN THE HOUSE ON Barnes Road was built. There are no photos of the carpenters or concrete workers who constructed the simple two-bedroom structure. All I know is it had a little driveway for the bright red Fiat, which would provide a Coloured family of five a rare freedom.

2

ON JULY 12, 1970, MY BROTHER THURN WAS born, cementing my mother and father's union with a tangible token of their hope. Eleven months later, to the day, I entered the world. Tania, their final child, was born on my parents' third wedding anniversary.

As my mother tells it, life glimmered with possibility. Though South Africa in the 1970s was still mired in Apartheid, my parents saw that men had walked on the moon and that people of their own age were influencing music, politics, science, and social change. They had no idea when—or even if—Apartheid would end, but in those days, there was more than just a scent of wishful thinking drifting across the land.

FATHER'S DAY JOB IS THAT OF A GLAZIER, CUTTING glass for commercial contracts. It is a good job to have in a Coloured community, and he is patient and meticulous. He comes home nightly, sometimes with nicks and cuts on his hands and arms. My mother carefully cleans his wounds as my father recounts his day's work. He has a way of making the mundane sound fanciful. He talks us through daydreams of faraway places where there were no arbitrary racial restrictions.

"It would be wonderful if we could move to England," he says. "I could find better work, and there would be more opportunities for the children," he says. Mummy daubs gently with her tweezers and cotton ball, smiling as she listens.

I marvel at the world Father shares with us from books he has read. He describes the green grass that covers the English land for miles, and the music that sounds through London's streets: The Beatles, Moody Blues, The Who, Don McLean. Yes, this is "honky" music, but Mummy thinks it more likely Londoners are listening to R&B than The Who.

"But how would we get visas out of here?" Mummy asks. "The government will never let us Coloureds out."

"We will find a way," Father says.

They talk like this into the night.

Our family of five goes for frequent walks through the neighborhood. Whether it is a daytime or evening walk, old Mrs. Bougaard, who lives next door, is a permanent fixture. Her arms are always folded under her bosom as she hangs over her Dutchdoor, watching the world pass by. I have only ever seen the top half of her body. She smiles and greets us as we pass by her house, and my mother says, "There is the Gossip Queen."

"Now, Lorraine. We mustn't talk bad about other people," Father says.

"*Eish!* She is the one always skinnering about everybody else in the neighborhood."

My father doesn't disagree. "Yes," he says, "but let's not do the same."

FATHER WAS MORE TROUBLED BY A PERSON'S PAIN than by the inequities of a country. Nobody was ever invisible to him. Sometimes he would bring a sick man or woman food cooked by my mother or read to a lonely soul, providing company and an escape. Other times, people sought him out as a neutral party to help intervene in a family overcome with emotional turbulence. He didn't seek out troubled situations, but he seemed to intuit sadness or difficulty in the people around him. He would often stop by neighborhood homes, sometimes simply to check in and say hello, sometimes to inquire as to the whereabouts of someone he thought might be straying from the right path, always to see how he might help.

"HOWZIT CYNTHIA, IS OWEN HOME?"

"*Ag*, no man, Edgar. That rubbish is never here! Check the tearoom. He's probably outside there with the corner boys getting drunk."

"I just came from there, and I did not see him."

"*Eish*! I don't know why I put up with him. He should be working and taking care of his children, but you know he drinks all his money away."

"Is it? When I see him, I'll sit him down, and we'll have a good talk. When you see Owen, tell him to come by my place."

"You are a good man, Edgar. How lucky your family is to have a good, hardworking man around the house."

FATHER STOPS TO TALK TO NELSON, A YARD BOY who works for a neighbor.

"How are you doing today, Nelson?"

"Not good, my brother."

"Tell me what is on your mind, Nelson. How can I help?"

"My brother, I wish it was something you could do. You know the situation of my peoples. It is not needed for the government to treat Black peoples like foreigners and what-what-what. Today, on my way here, I had to show the policeman my *dompas*. For what? For walking in my own land."

Father shakes his head. He understands. "There must be a purpose even in this madness."

FATHER MOVED WITH A PURPOSE THAT WAS OUT OF step with provincial backwater Apartheid. Even as we Coloureds lived under the shadow of a nonsensically brutal and racist system, Father's eyes were constantly on the horizon, looking toward the light, drinking in the crimsons, purples and burnt oranges of the skies.

He was keenly aware of the ways in which colors and people interacted, complemented each other, even leaned on one another.

At night, during his "periodic bursts of artistic productivity," as Mummy described them, Thurn, Tania, and I would watch him paint magnificent African sunsets of blue and gold. Sometimes Father would move his head next to mine, and we would apprise his efforts together. The warmth and beauty of the colors transfixed me.

Father always said, "Remember, my children—Black, White, Coloured, boy, girl—we are all simply people. If only men would look into the world rather than away from it."

I loved hearing him, even when his sayings left me confused. How can I have my feet on the ground and my head in the sky? How can someone look at the sky and look away from it at the same time?

None of this made sense to me at almost four years old, and I still wonder about it today.

One of my favorite paintings of his is a romanticized piece of my siblings and me, where Father uses bold horizontal brush strokes showcasing us children in what seems to be a French revolutionary era. I am perched on a piano draped with a loosely flowing cover smiling down at Tania, who sits on a wooden stool below me as if listening to a story I am sharing with her. To my left, Thurn stands with both his hands placed on his hips as he smiles with wide round eyes. There is an idealized innocence in my carefree sitting position with left knee tented and arms loosely wrapped around it, the right leg dangling freely from the piano. By the time I was in pre-school, I had fallen completely in love with my father. I sometimes wished to have him all to myself, a wish I confessed to no one else. I had a secret plan. We would marry and live in a little house on a big piece of land with fields of strawberries. We would spend all of our time in the sun picking our little heart-shaped fuzzy fruits.

It would be wonderful.

Maybe I wished to have him to myself as a way to separate myself from Tania, who, when we were younger, followed me everywhere. Until we started school, I did not mind. It was fun having an admirer. And, it was to my advantage. "If you want to play outside with me, we're skipping first, hopscotch second, and then we are picking flowers to stick on our fingernails, or I'm playing by myself." Tania and I both enjoyed picking flower petals from the Canna Lily with its long, bright red flowers that looked so elegant on our nails. We would each pick ten petals, then lick each fingernail and carefully stick the flowers on. Our elegant "nails" never stayed on very long because spit dries quickly, but for a couple of careful minutes, we were *laanies*. "Okay, fine," she would say.

Tania wished to please, and she had a blameless innocence about her. If I ever got upset, she would say, "please don't be mad at me, Gillian." Or, if she did not hear or understand what I or someone else was telling her, she would politely say, "I beg your pardon," just as we were taught to say to elders. Grown-ups found Tania impressive and would frequently say, "what a polite child." "If only all children were so mannerly." I rarely begged anyone's pardon.

AS SOON AS SCHOOL BEGAN FOR US BOTH, TANIA'S following me around did not feel so mannerly. I wanted to identify myself as separate from her. I did not wish to appear weak in front of my peers. Kids can be cruel with teasing, and I became cruel before others did. At lunchtime, I would hide behind a tree or a building while Tania looked for me. When she had given up, I would sneak out to my friends. Instead of feeling sorry for her, the frenzied look on her face as she searched brought only annoyance. One day I remember thinking, "God, why can't she go find her own friends to play with!" I immediately felt bad for using God's name in vain and pleaded His forgiveness that day, but I never asked forgiveness from hiding from Tania at school.

By this time, I had grown impatient with Tania's inobtrusive and accepting nature, so like Mummy's. Father's creativity and his insightful musings spoke more to me. My mother had reacted to the madness of Apartheid that surrounded us by disappearing. I saw this as surrender. My father, on the other hand, saw the madness as a tool to make one stronger. One of his favorite sayings came from Kahlil Gibran's *The Prophet*: "Out of suffering have emerged the strongest souls; the most massive characters are seared with scars." To Father, there was purpose in everything, even madness.

To me, he was the smartest human in the world.

Concrete memories of him are few and live as fleeting moments in time, disconnected from a larger narrative. Two memories I have are both from when I was very young, perhaps three years old. In one, I did something wrong. In another, I did something childish. In both memories, I disappointed him.

FATHER IS WASHING TANIA AND ME IN THE TUB. I have to pee, and instead of telling him I need to go to the toilet, I let it out in the bathtub. When Father asks who did it, I say, "It wasn't me," but Father replies, "Gillian, your voice does not sound like it is being honest." I freeze in disbelief, and then I burst into tears.

I AM STANDING IN THE CEMENT DRIVEWAY OUTside our home, anxiously awaiting his return. It is evening and pouring with rain. Rain is soaking through my clothing and matting my hair, but I hardly notice, nor do I flinch at the thunder and lightning cracking open the sky. Father will be home soon, and we will watch the storm together from the comfort of our little home while he tells me stories. To me, the sound of his voice is the best story in the world, and tonight I want to be the first person to greet him. To say "Hi, Daddy" before Mummy, Thurn, or Tania. So I stand outside in the rain.

Before long, I watch as the Fiat slowly pulls into the driveway. A giant smile covers my face. The wet soaking through to my skin, I feel like a drowning princess about to be rescued by her prince. I run toward the car.

But when the car stops and my father steps out into the rain, it's not the majestic welcome I am expecting. He yells, "Gillian, what are you doing out here?" His voice is sharp. "Go inside!"

Stung by the rare rebuke from this man I so idolize, I turn away from his car and run inside.

LOOKING BACK AS AN ADULT WITH TWO CHILDREN of my own, it seems obvious to me why my father was not thrilled to see his three-year-old daughter outside, alone on the driveway, soaked in a thunderstorm. Yes, you may say, but instead of speaking so sharply to you, couldn't he have swept you into his arms and carried you inside? How could he not have seen how happy you were to see him, even in the dark of a storm? Perhaps. But I'm sure he was afraid of how close he might have come to hitting me with the car. And in the storm, my flushed cheeks and bright eyes could have been confused for fever as much as for excitement. After all, Coloured children were far more likely to die of illness than White children. Even a fever could be dangerous for a Coloured child of my age and in that time. Whatever the reason for his scolding, Father was so upset, and I knew I must have done something wrong. And in my memory, when I run into our home on Barnes Road, I am running to the safest place I know.

3

PEOPLE THINK CHILDREN DON'T PAY ATTENtion, but they do. And sometimes they remember more than they would like to.

Of course, there are some things I don't remember about the day Aunty Alvia took Tania and me to the park, and Thurn was left at home, and there is much I don't remember about the days that followed. But before I tell you of that day at the park, let me tell you of another day a few weeks earlier. The day our family went to visit our father at a "resting place." It is the best I can offer by way of explanation for the events that followed.

It was December, the height of Durban summer, and Mother had dressed Tania and me in overall shorts and white, knee-high bobby socks. She often dressed us alike, and as a result, people who didn't know us sometimes thought we were twins, despite Tania having darker hair and slightly darker skin tone than me. Our overalls were off-white, featuring large colorful cartoon prints on the bib. Tania's had a picture of Snoopy holding his arms out as if he were going to give you a big hug. On mine, Donald Duck was wearing a blue sailor blouse and hat with his orange-yellow bill. He was smiling bigger than Snoopy.

Mummy and Granny told us we were going to visit Father in a place that looked like a hospital but was not a hospital. They said it was not a place for people with broken legs or arms, and they said he was not sick. He was just resting at this place for a little bit. Above all, we were to tell no one and "*always* keep family matters private."

The resting place was big and had lots of rooms in it. The walls were colorless. Even the air felt grey. It was unlike any place I'd ever been, and it scared me because it didn't feel like the kind of place anyone would want to go and rest. Nobody there smiled. Even Mummy and Granny looked serious. I remember noticing the smiling cartoon characters on the bibs of my and Tania's overalls and thinking it did not seem like the right place for Donald and Snoopy to look so happy.

When Father came home, we children were instructed not to ask him any questions about his resting place. And of course we didn't. At least I didn't.

For weeks after his return, Father mostly stayed at home. Because he was still resting, my Uncle Nicki, Mummy's youngest brother, came to visit, and whenever Mummy needed to go somewhere, Uncle Nicki would drive her in Father's car. When Father would leave the house, he would walk. One day he said he was going to walk to the tearoom, and I asked if I could go with him, but Mummy said no. I remember he returned a while later with a small sack of potatoes.

And this is all you need to know to understand what happened the day Tania and I were taken to the park.

I AM SHAKEN AWAKE BY AUNTY ALVIA, STANDING beside me. I hear frenzied footsteps and muffled crying.

"You must wake up," she says. "Come, get dressed, we are going to the park."

The footsteps. The crying. Aunty Alvia's voice does not sound like it is being honest.

I seek out the eyes of Thurn and Tania in the little room we share, looking for an answer, or maybe just comfort. I get neither.

"Come, we must go now!" Aunty Alvia says again, handing us some daytime clothes. "Here, put these on."

I can hear Mrs. Bougaard's voice in the next room. I begin to feel scared. Why is she inside our house and not hanging over her Dutchdoor? I strain to make out her words, but her voice is too soft. All I can hear is Aunty Alvia saying, "Hurry up" and "We must go now."

Within minutes Aunty Alvia is hurrying Tania and me down the street toward the park. My stomach is so full of butterflies; I feel they might lift me up and carry me away.

We arrive. I should be excited to ride on the merry-go-round or play with the other children, but I don't feel like playing today. I stand to one side and watch the children spin and sing:

> *Ring-a-ring o' roses,*
> *A pocket full of posies,*
> *A-tishoo! A-tishoo!*
> *We all fall down.*

I turn to Aunt Alvia. "When are we going home?" I ask.

"Just now." She does not look down.

"But I want to go *now now*. I want to see Mummy and Daddy."

"They're busy right now."

"Can I be busy with them?"

"No. You must be good. They are very busy."

"When will they stop being busy so I can go home?"

She doesn't answer.

After what feels like all day, we finally leave the park, and when we get home, only Mummy, Thurn, and a few family members are there. Father is not amongst them.

I WOULD LATER ASK THURN ABOUT HIS OWN MEMories of the day our father disappeared, and he would recall not being taken to the park with Tania and me. Instead, he remained at home and watched a black bag being carried into an ambulance. Why Tania and I were removed from the commotion of that morning, but Thurn was left at home, is still not clear today.

I developed the habit of finding activities that would put me in close proximity to adult conversation. I would select a book or catch beanbags, anything for an excuse to situate myself near enough to the adults so I could hear them talk, but far enough away that they had the impression I was playing alone. Then, feigning total preoccupation with my book or beanbag, I would listen to the conversations around me. When they thought I wasn't paying attention, that's when they would say things I was not supposed to hear.

"AG SHAME, MAN. IT'S SO TERRIBLE."

"*Ja*, I heard. Asphyxiation, right?"

"*Ja!*"

I hear them say how terrible this "fixation" is. Maybe fix Asian? I don't know.

All I know is that Father is gone.

WE EAT THE POTATOES FATHER BROUGHT BACK from the tearoom. Maybe he will come back to bring us more. The potatoes are gone, and he still has not come home. I know he is somewhere, I just don't know where.

"Your mother is not doing very well right now. Go play outside."

Our house now holds four people, not five, and at school, when I write the number 5 on a piece of paper, it looks unfamiliar, like a bizarre letter S, no matter how long I look at it. My teacher gets mad at me. She says, "Last week you could write the number 5, why can't you now?" I don't know how to answer her. Maybe it is because Father taught me how to last week and this week he is not at home.

I want to ask about this fixation or fix Asian or whatever it is, but questions are not allowed. When I ask where he is and when he will be coming home, the answers tell me nothing.

"Don't ask questions unless an adult addresses you first."

I'm a quick learner, so it's not long before I under-stand "speak when spoken to" is now the most important rule in our home.

"You must not ask such questions. Speak when spo-ken to."

Thurn asks a question, and punishment is swift. I watch as Sunlight soap is shoved in his mouth, and I watch as tears roll down his face, the thick bar of green soap sticking out between his lips.

"This is not a discussion for now, so mind your man-ners, young lady."

I keep my mouth closed, and my burning questions to myself.

I am three and one-half years old.

YEARS LATER, I WOULD PIECE TOGETHER FROM FAM-ily members further details of that day: that my father suffered from depression and was later diagnosed with schizophrenia; that Mummy believed the medication he was given for depression led to symptoms mimicking schizophrenia; that whatever his diagnosis, he suffered enough to slip into our family car, that tireless red Fiat, as it whuffed in park for hours and sent him into the unknown.

I wonder about the route he took prior to getting into the car. Was it the journey of Ulysses as he navigated past the sofa, the well-worn chair, the paintings on the wall—his paintings? Did he drift on some tide through the living room, taking one final look around, glancing at his beloved books on the table, his eyes grazing the doily-covered arms of the sofa? Did he open the cabinets of the kitchen to see the food he would never eat? Did he stand in the doorway of the room I shared with Thurn and Tania and listen to us breathing? Or did he enter our room to lay soft kisses of goodbye and regret on our foreheads—a final farewell? Did he think of us at all as he walked out of our home forever and closed the door behind him?

Our house on Barnes Road may be there still, but for decades now, I've visited it only in my dreams. If I were inclined to believe in haunted houses, I would say this surely was one, and its ghosts have stayed with me since I left, following me from house to house throughout the years. Some of those ghosts have been benevolent, others malignant; some may be drifting through the house I live in right now, where I write these words, like a wisp of cloud in the wind—or, if life shows its meaning in patterns, like a stolen caul.

4

JUST AS SUDDENLY AS FATHER WENT AWAY, WE were taken to live with Granny and Uncle Johnny— three children, a couple of bags, a quick goodbye, a getaway car, and Mummy was gone.

"Granny," as we called her, was my mother's mother, and Uncle Johnny, her second husband and the only man whose company she loved to be in. It was with him that Granny found some peace and happiness, though some in the family called them a terrible match. Aunty Val, Granny's oldest, was most unhappy about their union and frequently vented her dissatisfaction to my mother.

"Mummy is too beautiful to be with a bladdy Hottentot."

"Come on, Val, we must be nice to Uncle Johnny. He's not terribly bad."

"What? Bladdy hell he is. The man does not even have two ½ cents to rub together. *Ay!* Another thing, too. He is *not* my uncle. He's just bladdy well Mr. Foster."

"*Ja,* but he makes Mummy happy."

"I don't know why. He was married to a drunk, left high and dry strumming his guitar on a park bench, *and* the man is from bladdy God knows where!"

Granny was indeed a beautiful woman. She was half African, born to the granddaughter of a Zulu chief who once ruled a good portion of Southern Africa. With fair skin, bright green eyes, and fine features, she resembled the Welsh father she never knew. Given that he was a White man who impregnated a Coloured woman, little was known of him. Whether their relationship was a casual fling or a full-blown love affair, it was prohibited under Apartheid. So his sole legacy within the family was Granny, her sister, and a single picture of him, which portrays a well-groomed European man, sitting Britishly stiff and inscrutable in his chair.

Uncle Johnny was a short man, perhaps 5′4″ tall, with yellow-brown skin and stubby, kinky hair cut close to his head. He wore a permanent smile affixed to his face—a smile common among subservient Black South Africans, an obsequious mask to give the appearance of meaning no harm or offense to any person, a shield to protect oneself from inadvertent anger or blame, just as the familiar "yessah" does in the American South. He was a simple man, and, like my father, he was always ready with a quote, though his were far less profound: "Put a smile on your dial and make someone's day!" Or another of his repeated favorites, "Where you are, I once was, and where I am, you will soon be."

Not many of us in the family paid attention to his proverbs, and the moment he began speaking always seemed to coincide with a game of musical chairs, with the loser being seated next to him and forced to listen to how many times one should chew their food before swallowing. Still, he loved Granny, and unlike her first husband, who abused her regularly, Uncle Johnny worshipped the ground she walked on.

Granny and Uncle Johnny lived in a tiny cement basement that was part of a larger dwelling located in a Coloured community called Greenwood Park. The main portion of the house belonged to the Haines family, a couple with a son named David. During the time we stayed with Granny, David's father would die from cancer, and he and his mother remained in the upstairs part of the house while Granny, Uncle Johnny, and us three children continued to live in the basement.

The basement unit felt more like a cave than anything else. Though it was just one bedroom, it had been subdivided into three makeshift rooms: a narrow bedroom, a tiny living room, and a kitchen that fit precisely two people before becoming overcrowded. The bedroom had two beds: one firmly placed against the back wall, with a small window perched above it allowing for a little morning light to enter—this was where Granny and Uncle Johnny slept—and a trundle bed that turned into a couch during daylight hours. This is where Thurn, Tania, and I slept.

The whistling tea kettle at Granny Foster's house woke me each morning to murmured conversation from the kitchen and the smell of tea in the air. Like many European traditions, the Dutch and British exported the cultural habit of drinking tea to South Africa, where it is now drunk on a regular basis. But of course, it isn't without a South African take on it: strong, piping hot, sweetened and lightened to a creamy color with heaped teaspoons of condensed milk. At least this is how Granny made it for us.

Lying in bed, I would listen to the sound of the tea kettle's screech, then the water being poured into a waiting cup, followed by the bright cling of a teaspoon: the sounds of Granny preparing Uncle Johnny's tea before he left for work. Though I was never aware of the exact time of the first kettle's whistle, I knew it was early because it was still dark. When the stirring ceased, I would burrow my way back to sleep under snug covers. Even as a child, I had a profound appreciation for sleep; I never had to be coaxed to go to bed, and certainly never to stay in bed; I imagine this came from Granny, who always referred to sleep as her "only consolation in life." I found great comfort in shut-eyes. They smoothed out the sharp edges of life, if only temporarily—and my life had many sharp edges.

When the second teapot whistle screeched, it was our cue to get up. I quickly made my way out of the rollout bed I shared with Tania and Thurn and raced to the tiny kitchen. The steaming cups of morning milky sweet tea were always there, and I came to appreciate the comfort of the ritual. Flavorful, warm, comforting, morning tea became a bellwether of consistency following Father's disappearance.

Another hallmark of Granny's house, though not as comforting, was the smell of fumigated Dettol, a liquid antiseptic and disinfectant Granny used on everything: If we had a cut, she applied Dettol to it; if countertops were dirty, she wiped them down with diluted Dettol; if anyone was sick, she added Dettol to their bathwater. Granny found many uses for Dettol, along with her other favorite antiseptic, TCP. The combination of the two created a profoundly sterile smell in the tiny—but spotless—basement.

One of my chores while living with Granny was to polish the few silver ornaments and teapot she kept in a glass cabinet. She took great pride in her few possessions, and in turn, I took pride in polishing her treasures, carefully burnishing each piece with a cloth until I could clearly see my reflection on the surface.

While polishing one day, I was caught short by the sight of my face in the teapot. It was so startling that I stopped, staring back at myself for a long while. The shocking thing about the face blinking back at me was not how different I looked, but how much the same. So much in my world had changed, and yet there I was, just the same as before, the same tight curls framing the same round face, the only difference a new, perplexed expression staring back at me.

At four o'clock every afternoon, Tania, Thurn, and I took turns washing our bodies in the small washroom built onto the outside of the house. It was really nothing more than a cement cube. In it was a tin bucket we used as our bathtub. Though there was plumbing, that did not mean we had hot running water; boiling water from the kitchen stove was mixed with cold water from the single faucet in the makeshift washroom that Granny poured into the bucket. Wooden swinging doors, just like old saloon doors, were attached midway up the cement walls, allowing for some privacy, though our legs and head could always be seen from the outside when standing upright in the tub.

There was no toilet in the washroom. If we needed to go to the bathroom, we ventured several feet down a slope from the main house, through a dense thicket of brush and trees, to an outhouse. The outhouse was a scary place; I often found spiders creating elaborate webs, which I was certain could trap me. I feared these critters so much that I learned to hold my pee, finally going to the outhouse only when absolutely necessary. Even then, I took a broom to defend myself against whatever critter might have mistaken the toilet for their home—or me for a potential meal.

My fear wasn't completely unfounded: though most of the insects I encountered were harmless, South Africa's KwaZulu-Natal region has more than its share of venomous bugs and snakes. Granny kept the path leading to the outhouse scrupulously clear of brush, using a bush knife—comparable to a machete, but designed for harvesting sugarcane—to chop away at the giant weeds and wild vegetation growing around her house. Still, not knowing what might slither out of the surrounding wilds, I was always acutely cautious.

IT IS A TYPICALLY HOT AND HUMID NATAL DAY, AND I stand looking down on Granny as she whacks away at the growth below. I stand on a cement area that serves as Granny's outdoor laundry space, where she washes our clothes by hand, pressing each item against an angled slab of cement to help her scrub. Her arthritic fingers are always bone stiff when she is through, but the clothes are immaculate. I lean on the dry slab and watch Granny hack at the bush along the pathway.

"Watch carefully now," she says. "Soon, you children are going to have to help chopping this bush."

I shiver at the idea of one day having to do this chore. If scary bugs live in the outhouse, what kind of creatures live in the bushes? I reassure myself we will only be living with Granny for a short while, so short we won't be here by the time of the next cutting. This has to be true.

Suddenly, Granny starts yelling, "*Inyonka! Inyonka!*" and slashes her huge bush knife into the wild brush over and over again. I have no idea what is happening and absolutely no idea what she is saying. My first thought is that she is yelling at the bush because she is mad at having to do all this work—but then a piece of snake flies into the air, and I want to run, but it all happens so quickly, even if I'd been able to move, I wouldn't have had time to run. Granny keeps slashing at the bush like a mad person; then she stops, takes a breath, and looks up at me. She wipes her forehead with the arm holding the now-bloody bush knife, and shouts, "Good thing it was not a bladdy mamba! Those things will kill you!"

Later I ask Granny what she yelled at the snake. She says it was Zulu, the language of "coons" and "kaffirs." Granny is half Zulu herself, but we know never to act Black. Yet, when she is startled or angry, there is no mistaking the Zulu within her.

GRANNY GREW UP ON A RURAL FARM IN NONGIDI, under the careful eye of her two doting grandmothers, Gertrude Ubutea Fynn and Christine Mkhiza, who called her by her Zulu name: Nomawala. They lived on the banks of the Mtwavuna River, the boundary line between the old colonial Pondoland and Natal. African legend held that the water spirits carried away anyone who did not confess their sins before crossing the Mtwavuna River. As a little girl, Granny would fetch water from the river, and wash clothing, bathe, and play in the shallow waters. The river, which flows into the Indian Ocean, never carried her off. To my mind, this was proof she'd confessed her sins before it, whatever they might have been.

Granny's marriage to her first husband and my grandfather, David Tucker, was an arranged one. To say their union was unpleasant would be an undeserved kindness to David Tucker.

As I would later learn, Grandpa David was a troubled man who never missed a day of *ijuba*. Though *ijuba* comes in many forms, it was always cheap—the cheapest form of alcohol in South Africa. I was never around Grandpa David much, as my grandparents divorced early in my childhood, but whenever I did see him, I kept my distance. His eyes were permanently blood-flecked and weepy, and when he spoke, he slurred in a wave of stale, sour breath. He had dark, shriveled skin that had seen too much of life, and his hair gave the appearance of several layers of grease as if he had never known the pleasure of a bath.

Some family members called him "*Doomakanda,*" Zulu for hard head. Mummy always referred to him as "Come Friday," because Monday through Thursday he worked as a molder for Metal Foundries in Durban, South Africa, but come Friday, he would comb back his greasy hair, put on a sleek suit, and step out into the Durban tropical night to drink and gamble his hard-earned money away.

Granny and David Tucker had six children together. Their youngest, Monica, was seven years old when Granny sent her out one evening to find David.

"Go fetch your father and tell him to come home for supper," Granny told Monica.

Monica found David Tucker sitting on a porch drinking with friends. She walked toward him to say it was time to come home for supper. She must have seen him look up at her through glassy eyes as she approached the curb because the family talked about how David Tucker saw the car that hit and killed his youngest daughter the instant she stepped into the street.

Granny never forgave David Tucker for Monica's death. She had put up with years of verbal and physical abuse from a drunken husband with empty pockets, but as far as she was concerned, had he been home instead of gambling and drinking, then Monica would be alive.

On a particular Saturday, Granny got dressed up and marched to St. Theresa's Church in Durban, where she

was a faithful attendee at Sunday Mass. She had sched-
uled a meeting with Father Roots, the priest of St. Theresa's. She arrived early, as she always did for appointments,
and was welcomed by Father Roots.

"Hello, Mrs. Tucker! Tell me, what brings you in to see
me outside of Mass?"

"Let me not waste the church's time," she said. "I am
not one to mince my words, so I will get straight to the
point. I am here because I have given much thought to
the serious matter before me, and I would like to ask the
church to grant me a divorce from my husband, David
Tucker."

"But Mrs. Tucker," Father Roots said, "I regret to
inform you a divorce from your husband is not possible.
You see, the Bible says, as a woman and as a wife, you
must submit yourself unto your husband, as unto the
Lord. And if you so choose to go against the commands
of the Lord, I am sorry to say but you will not be permitted through God's holy doors on Sundays. Let me read
to you, Ephesians 5:22–5:24: 'For the husband is the head
of the wife, even as Christ is the head of the church: and
he is the savior of the body. Therefore, as the church is
subject unto Christ, so [let] the wives [be] to their own
husbands in everything.'"

As biblical verses rolled off his tongue, Father Roots
could not have known that all the holy words in the
world would not change Granny's mind. It had been
made up before she even entered the church that day.
Her meeting with Father Roots was simply a formality, a
token of respect to the Lord. Neither could Granny have

known that in less than a year, Father Roots would over-see the burial of her son-in-law. And no one could have predicted that the priest who would not give Granny her divorce from David Tucker would subsequently impregnate a married woman from Sydenham, and the two would flee to Belgium.

By the end of that Saturday, David's bags were packed, divorce papers filed, and Granny knelt down at her bed with her rosary in hand and prayed for forgiveness.

MUMMY BREEZES INTO GRANNY'S HOUSE FOR ONE of her infrequent visits, like a movie star making a cameo appearance. Her smooth brown skin reflects the light in a way that makes her glow. Her hair is straight and neatly combed, and her eyebrows are plucked into thin black lines. She stays for a short while, then slips quietly out the back door like mist. I watch as she walks quickly down the slope leading to the outhouse, and I think that maybe she just needs to use the toilet, but at the outhouse, Mummy makes a sharp turn through the bush. Before she is able to make her getaway, however, Tania has run after her and grabbed onto Mummy's dress. Clinging to her with a vice-grip, she wails, "Please don't leave me, please, please, Mummy!"

Granny hollers from the house, "Tania, get back inside right now!"

But Tania pays no mind to Granny and refuses to let Mummy go. Realizing she needs to use another approach,

Granny marches to her outdoor laundry area and grabs a hanger from the clothesline above her. Then she hollers again, "Tania, if you don't let go of your mother, I will hit you with this hanger!" Tania immediately lets go, Granny swoops down on Tania like a hawk and scoops her up while Mummy runs free. Mummy doesn't look back as she disappears through the trees.

Tania's emotional outburst at Mummy's leaving surprises me. It seems to me she is causing a lot of unnecessary commotion and trouble for everyone. I wish she would stop.

YOU MAY WONDER AT MY REACTION, BUT I WAS JUST a child myself. And in those days, children minded their elders. Thurn, Tania, and I had been told never to discuss our father's disappearance, so we didn't. Mummy had left us in Granny's care to live in her one-bedroom basement, so we did not speculate as to why Mummy had become nothing more than a fluttering presence in our lives.

But though I didn't question these things, I absorbed every detail of them.

I have always been a keen observer with a memory for the minutiae of a moment: white sheets dusted with sand the colour of my skin, a crack in a glass, passing conversations (*Ag, no man, Edgar. That rubbish is never here!*). My daughter Kiara is the same way. She can recall what clothing someone was wearing on a certain day a year before, and if she meets you once, she will never forget your name.

So though I could have been no more than five, I remember quite clearly watching Granny with keen eyes as she went about the daily tasks of life in her tiny basement home. I remember the way her arthritic fingers clawed around the handle of the kettle as she poured hot water into a teapot filled with leaves. I watched as she covered the pot with a hand-stitched tea cozy. Granny was a fine seamstress, and I loved to watch her thread needles, sew buttons, and knit. On Sundays, I saw for myself as she transformed herself into the perfect lady. She would powder her nose, slip on a pretty dress and high-heeled shoes, and look very beautiful and dignified. Though I loved watching her sew and dress up and do all the things she said a lady must do to manage a house, I had no patience for those things myself. I preferred bare feet over shoes, trousers over dresses, and I didn't concern myself with taming my unruly curls. My behavior drove Granny to distraction.

"*Ag*, Gillian, you must not slouch, a lady walks with her head high and her shoulders straight. And cross your legs when you sit. Ladies sit properly—never with their legs open. You hear me?"

My curls were a source of constant frustration for Granny. I preferred to keep my hair loose, and I didn't mind if it held on to bits of leaves from a tree I'd climbed or sand from a beach we visited; these were souvenirs from my outdoor adventures. Granny insisted on keeping my hair knot and souvenir free.

IT'S BREAKFAST TIME, AND I'M STANDING IN THE living room, and Granny is combing the knots out of my hair. I squirm as she rakes the comb through my hair. "Stand still and eat your porridge before it gets cold!" she scolds. I stare at my bowl of Jungle Oats and the dollop of melted butter on its surface, but all I can think of is the pain as Granny yanks at the knots in my thick curls, like a fisherman trying to pull in an oversized catch. With every brushstroke, it feels like she is uprooting my hair from the scalp. As much as I want to obey her orders and stay still and eat my porridge, the pain is just too much. I pull away from her and let out a loud cry.

Granny loses all patience and forgets about being a lady. "I don't have time for this nonsense, Gillian!" and she pushes my head from behind, thrusting my face into my bowl of porridge. It doesn't hurt, the porridge has cooled by now, but it does shock the living daylights out of me. I let out a cry so loud Granny drops the comb she is holding. She runs to the kitchen and comes scurrying back with a damp towel.

"I am so sorry, my Gillian," she says. She wipes the mask of porridge, snot, and tears from my face. Rushing back to the kitchen, she returns with a piece of candy.

"Here, my child, please forgive Granny."

5

WE LIVED WITH GRANNY AND UNCLE JOHNNY for two years. Tania eventually stopped crying for Mummy, and Thurn retreated into a world of his own. At some point after Father disappeared, Thurn stopped smiling and became even more of a question mark to me than before. He never talked much except to ask obvious questions like, "What are you doing?" This annoyed me because if I'm playing hopscotch, then it's obvious what I am doing. But I would just say, "playing hopscotch" or "I'm sweeping the floor" because I didn't want to upset him. He had become terribly sensitive, and if I said, "Can't you see what I am doing?" he would get most upset. Sometimes he would play hide-and-go-seek with Tania and me, but mostly he just kept to himself. When Granny told me that I must teach Thurn how to read by reading to him in the afternoons because he was having trouble with this subject, Thurn, who was a year older than me, was not happy. But we both had to obey Granny or else we wouldn't get to listen to stories on Springbok radio in the evenings.

Days began with morning tea followed by a list of responsibilities, which included clearing the brush around the outhouse with Granny's bush knife, learning how to sew, and polishing Granny's ornaments. Leisure hours were spent sitting under the lychee tree, eating the sweet fleshy fruits until our stomachs couldn't take any more.

One of my least favorite jobs was helping Granny clean jackfruit to make jackfruit curry, the most awful-tasting thing in the world. Unfortunately, the gigantic, musky-smelling fruit grew plentifully in the yard and made an inexpensive meal. Using her bush knife, Granny would chop the jackfruit into sticky chunks, then cook it with tomatoes and spices. The smell alone made me nauseous.

My other main responsibility was spinach picking.

When Granny needed spinach for dinner, she handed Tania and me a used plastic shopping bag and sent us out. Spinach grew wild in Greenwood Park and could be found sprouting between cement cracks, on the side of roads, and in empty spaces.

"Only Indians pick wild spinach," a kid from the neighborhood told us one day, and after that, Tania and I were embarrassed to go out picking. Still, we didn't have a choice—when Granny told us to do something, her instructions outweighed our embarrassment.

That didn't mean the shame went away, though, and Tania and I did our best to hide our spinach picking, sometimes using one another as the shield.

"You hold the bag."

"No, I held it when we left Granny's house."

"Don't think you are the boss just because you are one year older."

I snatched the bag of spinach from Tania's hands and shoved it under my top, pressing the air out so the bulge in my stomach was less noticeable. "Fine, but don't ask to play with me later on."

"That's not fair," Tania said.

"Well, Granny says life is not fair."

"What does that mean?"

"I don't boil my cabbages twice," I retorted. I'd picked this saying up from my grandmother; as near as I could tell, it meant thinking too hard about anything solved nothing.

I WAKE TO THE SOUND OF GRANNY MOVING AROUND in the kitchen. The tea kettle, which is normally my alarm, is quiet. For the first time in memory, Granny has not made morning tea. I slide out of the trundle bed I share with Thurn and Tania, my unruly blonde curls askew as always, and shuffle into the kitchen.

Granny is making sandwiches, cutting them carefully, wrapping them up in brown paper, and setting them in a box. "We have a long day ahead of us today," she says. "Go comb the knots out of your hair."

"Are we having a picnic?" I ask.

Granny places Oros—a concentrated, orange-flavored drink—and slices of buttered toast into a separate bag, then places the boxed sandwiches and quartered oranges in the bag with some serviettes. It looks as though there is food for all five of us.

"Are we having a picnic?" I ask again.

"Long day today, my Gillian," she says. "No more questions. Get your brother and sister up." As I go to wake up Thurn and Tania, I hear Granny take in a deep breath and let out a sigh behind me. I turn. She is still at the counter, but she has stopped packing the food, and I see her staring out the small kitchen window into the teeth of the sunrise. She shakes her head once, and then she begins to cut and pack once more.

Bags are neatly positioned at the door. I'm told we're going to be eating breakfast in Uncle Johnny's car. With eyes still heavy with sleep, Thurn, Tania, and I shuffle out the door to Uncle Johnny's shiny car, idling gently outside the house.

UNCLE JOHNNY LOVED HIS CAR. HE KEPT IT SPOT-less, polishing it religiously every Saturday, tending to every inch. When I watched him fuss over his car, I would occasionally remember our Fiat and wish that Father were back and taking care of us. This would lead me to wonder where Mummy had gone.

Thurn was never anywhere to be found on Saturdays, and since Tania and I didn't have the nerve to hide, we were bestowed the honor of helping Uncle Johnny polish his car, while he shared his philosophies on life.

"You see, Gillian and Tania, in life, if you take good care of anything, it will take good care of you. Take my car, for example. I take good care of it, and in turn, it takes care of us. Not many Coloured families can say they have a car, let alone one so nice."

I was not permitted to question, of course, but it seemed to me no matter how much a person took care of something, it could still break. Had Uncle Johnny already forgotten how his chariot broke down a few weeks ago while taking him to work? He had spent the day getting it to a garage so it could be fixed. It seemed to me Uncle Johnny spent all his time fussing over something that was eventually going to break down anyway. I just couldn't believe Uncle Johnny knew what he was talking about.

Uncle Johnny particularly annoyed Thurn. Thurn didn't like to talk or be bothered with anything, so when he would periodically voice complaints to Tania and me about Uncle Johnny, we knew he was really upset: "I don't understand. Why does he always have to chew his food so loud?" Thurn couldn't stand to hear anyone chew or swallow their food, especially Uncle Johnny. "How can someone make a crunching sound when eating plain bread?"

Once, when the chewing sounds became too great for Thurn, he had gotten up from the table and marched right out the door. This was a shock to me because such behavior from us children was never allowed.

AS GRANNY AND UNCLE JOHNNY LOAD US INTO THE car, Thurn asks, "Where are we going, Uncle Johnny?"

Uncle Johnny shoves a handful of bags into the car. "We are going to iFafa."

iFafa

6

IFAFA.

The word *iFafa* is Zulu in origin, meaning "sparkling," and it is the name of a small coastal town in Natal, South Africa, approximately one hundred kilometers from Durban. That is what Uncle Johnny tells us from his perch behind the wheel of his chariot as he drives us to this place with a name I have never heard of before.

Tania, Thurn, and I, still groggy with sleep, slouch in the back. I fight to keep my eyes open so I can watch where we are going. Uncle Johnny has stopped talking, and we drive in silence for what seems like a very long time. Then Granny's voice breaks the quiet.

"You children need to listen to me now," she says. "You are all three going to boarding school in iFafa. It is just your mother now since your father died. It is the best thing for everybody."

I sit upright. I am fully awake now. Shocked and more confused than ever, I open my mouth and speak without thinking: "When did—" but Granny quickly interrupts me.

"Now is not the time for questions. You need to listen. I want no crying. The people who will take care of you are good people. Do not give them any problems. You hear me?"

I want to cry, to beg, but I am scared to speak back to Granny. Or maybe I am too shocked to speak. Or maybe it is both. Whatever the reason, Thurn and Tania say nothing either. We know it won't do any good, and we will only make Granny mad.

I look out the window and notice for the first time we are in the middle of an electrical storm. My heart beats time with the wipers of the car. Granny continues to speak from the front passenger seat while keeping her eyes fixed in front of her. Her mouth moves. I hear nothing. I watch the rain run down the window, blurring the road I have never seen before.

I feel like the time at Umhlanga Rocks when a giant ocean wave knocked me over and sucked my body under, and no one could hear the bubbles coming out of my mouth. The frighteningly large Durban waves tossed me about and pulled me down as I fought for air, and I felt I was going to die. Somehow, I managed to pull myself out of the water, and I ran to tell Mummy about my near-death experience.

"Well, swim in the shallow end next time," she said.

The car pushes us through the rain and further and further from the shallow end of the ocean if there ever was one. Father is really gone now, Mummy is missing, and we are being sent to someplace called iFafa.

Lightning cracks in the sky above us.

Uncle Johnny looks back at Tania, Thurn, and me, our three heads silently bobbing in the back seat, and says, "Remember, you must always keep a smile on your dial."

Uncle Johnny's car seems to be made for going under the speed limit, and the drive is about two hours long. Very little is said. Eventually, the rain stops, and through the window, I see the occasional farmhouse but no signs of life.

Thurn is dropped off first.

We come to a full stop at a large farmhouse surrounded by fields stretching in every direction. There are no road signs, no landmarks, nothing to indicate where we are. I cannot see any neighbors, only a few mangy cows, some pigs, and chickens. Thurn says, "I thought we are going to boarding school?"

"This is boarding school, Sarg."

We emerge from the car into a cloud of dust. The roads, the sugarcane and mielie fields, even the car, normally cream in color, are covered with this orange-brown dust.

At the head of this property is an elderly Coloured couple, Mr. and Mrs. Goldstone. They seem nice enough people, and Mrs. Goldstone is very excited to see Granny. "*Ay,* Zoe!" she says, "I haven't seen you in donkey's years." Pleasantries are exchanged, and Thurn is shown to his room. "You will be sharing this room with another boy," Mrs. Goldstone says. I search the tidy room for the other boy, but nobody is there.

"There are two other boys who live here," Mrs. Goldstone continues. "Shawn is the oldest, so he has his own room. And all three of you will have chores to do—you hear me, my boy?"

Thurn nods in agreement. Whatever he is thinking does not show on his face.

I want to rest my head on one of the empty beds with sheets and blankets tightly tucked under their mattresses. Instead, I stand straight. Like a lady. I try not to cry.

"You see the yard boy out there?" and Mrs. Goldstone points out the window at a young African man working on the property. "His name is Tuesday, and he is not here to serve you," she chuckles. She speaks with firmness similar to Granny's, and when she talks, people listen. She commands respect, and I think she and Granny could be sisters in this way. I will find out later they are, in fact, cousins.

A few minutes later, an African woman wearing an apron, and a loosely tied scarf around her head, enters the room.

"Excuse me, Madam, but your tea is ready. I put it on the veranda just like you said."

As Granny and Mrs. Goldstone talk over tea, Tania and I are instructed to "go play in the yard." We remove ourselves, but neither of us is in the mood to play. Tania keeps close to my side as we walk around the farm.

"Are we also going to stay on a farm like this one?" Tania asks.

"I don't know."

"When do you think we will see Mummy?"

"I don't know."

"How long are we going to be here?"

"I don't know. Stop asking me so many questions."
I point in a random direction, as all directions are the
same, and say, "I'm going to walk over this way. I want
to be left alone."

"Well, I *don't* want to be left alone," Tania says, "and
Granny says we have to stay together."

"Fine then. But no talking."

"Okay, just don't leave me."

Everything around the farm seems to have been
there for a very long time. Rusting farm implements are
strewn about and half-buried in the ground, enveloped
by weeds and grass. Having lived only in the city, many
of these tools are unfamiliar to me. They look especially
dull yet exceptionally dangerous. Not far from the house
is a tin shack with a roof held down by rocks where the
servants live. Plastic containers of all shapes and sizes,
their tops cut off, are scattered about the farm; all of
them are partially filled with rainwater. Everything, even
the cows, look withered and old.

After aimlessly wandering for a while, Tania and
I make our way back to the main house. Granny and
Mrs. Goldstone have finished their tea but are still talking. They speak in Zulu, presumably so that we can't
understand them, but Tania and I sit and listen to the
heavy clicking sounds of their conversation anyway.

Once their secret conversation has ended, Tania and
I are shuffled back into the car, and Mrs. Goldstone bids
us farewell. Thurn stands on a small dirt bank near Mrs.
Goldstone, and as the car drives us away, he looks on,
but he doesn't wave goodbye.

I don't wave either. I just stare back at him, standing in front of the farmhouse, and watch the distance between us grow.

7

AFTER DRIVING FOR A WHILE, UNCLE JOHNNY turned up on a long dirt road that parts an endless green sea of sugarcane fields a shoulder high. At the top of the dirt lane sat a small house made of red bricks. A makeshift wire gate guarded the entrance of the property, and Uncle Johnny put the car in park as Granny got out to swing the gate open. She paused for a moment and looked at the house up ahead, then back at us with a short smile. I supposed she meant to be reassuring, but there was sadness in her smile. Granny returned to the passenger seat, Uncle Johnny put the car in gear, and we drove through the gate and toward the house.

Though the house itself was small, it sat on a large plot of land overlooking sprawling sugarcane fields. In the distance, I could see the vast, sparkling waters of the Indian Ocean. Tania and I would live here for the next two years, somewhere between secret conversations and distant waters.

Mr. and Mrs. Fayes were the owners of the little red house in the sugarcane farm. They were ordinary, pleasant people, nondescript in every way.

A boy about two years older than me also lived at the boarding school. He had his own room, while Tania and

I shared one. He was very private, but so were Tania and I, and we never interacted with him much except when we gathered around the kitchen table for meals. Even then, few words were exchanged.

In this corner of the world where continuous fields of sugarcane and long grass spread to the horizon, the closest neighbors were miles away. I could have climbed the tallest tree and looked in every direction and not seen another human being. This will be our new home.

In iFafa, there were two things to occupy our time: chores and school. The school itself was a simple one-story brick building with a handful of rooms for classes. The building was as lonely as everything else in this corner of the world—a simple structure sitting on red dirt in the middle of nowhere. The three-or-so-mile walk to school down dirt roads left my white socks brown.

One of our favorite pastimes was to hunt for mushrooms. After every thunderstorm, Tania and I would run outside with a basket, wandering far into the bush behind the farm, and pick as many mushrooms as we could find. Returning back to the farmhouse, Mrs. Faye would fry them in butter with a generous amount of salt and pepper. This treat was better than any Cadbury chocolate Granny had ever given me.

Mr. Fayes loved spicy food; each night, his meal was accompanied by a small bowl of peri-peri chiles, also known as "devil chiles." Historically found in the African wild, peri-peri grow to about the size of a bee, and eating one feels like you have been stung in the mouth. Mr. Faye ate them like candy, and Tania and I were assigned the chore of picking a small bowl for him before dinner each evening from the small bushes in the back yard. Simply picking the chiles would sting our fingers. Years later, I learned that Mr. Fayes died from stomach cancer. One can only wonder if this African Devil had anything to do with it.

There was no electricity at this little farmhouse on the hill. We used paraffin lamps at night, and dinner and chores were to be finished before darkness settled in. After sunset, I would often see a lamp flickering in the boy's room as he completed his homework, undoubtedly squinting to make out words in the dim light. The oil lamp Tania and I shared was to be used only to light the path to the washroom, where we brushed our teeth at the same time each night before going to sleep.

Outside of school and chores, Tania and I were left to our own devices. There were no cats to play with, no dogs to chase, no toys to entertain us. The only "toys" available were sticks, and playing with sticks came with its own hazards.

TANIA AND I ARE COMBING THE YARD LOOKING FOR twigs to play a game of pick-up-sticks. I have collected a handful of sticks when I see a long, especially smooth stick I must have missed, lying on the ground at my feet. "We won't have to use a knife to make this one smooth," I think, and I pick it up. Suddenly this smooth stick begins to fiercely wiggle in my hand. Realizing it's a snake, I fling both my hands open and sticks and snake fly in Tania's direction. She runs screaming inside the house, the snake slides away, and I am left wondering what possible game I can play by myself.

After making a mud cake and failing to persuade one of the pigs to join me for a tea party, I try to convince Tania to come back outside to play with me.

"If you come outside, I will let you choose whatever game you want to play."

"*No*, you threw a snake at me."

"It was an accident."

"No, it was not."

"Cross my heart, hope to die, stick a needle in my eye." I make the sign of the cross over my chest.

"No."

"Fine. I promise from now on, I will kick the sticks to make sure they don't wiggle before picking them up."

I don't remember if she came out to play with me again that day.

ASIDE FROM TANIA, DAYDREAMING WAS MY ONLY companion, and I used it to go to faraway places and create magical stories about a life I didn't have. I carried with me a picture I had found in an old magazine which Mrs. Fayes let me have. It was a picture of a lady wearing a bright yellow skirt. Though the lady in the picture was White (there were no African or Coloured people in that magazine), I cut it out because of her yellow skirt. Yellow was Mummy's favorite color, so I pretended this unknown White woman was Mummy, and I would smile and talk to her, and she always smiled back.

With all my daydreaming, how I passed my classes and moved to the next level, I don't know. My behavior kept me out of trouble, and my report cards gave the appearance of being on track, so people left me alone. I don't remember anything of what I learned at this boarding school in iFafa. What I remember most from those years is a lady wearing a bright yellow skirt who would smile at me when I went to bed at night and send me dreams of

> *blue, yellow, orange and green,*
> > *of shimmering violet and strawberry beams,*
> > > *of sunbeam hugs and rain-tickled kisses,*
> > > > *where lavender mist dances with gold mango*
> *wishes.*

I envied the little boy with whom we lived, whose family came every Friday and took him home for the weekend. No one ever came to fetch Tania and me for the weekend.

In iFafa, the sea and I were reintroduced.

Before Father's death, we often went to Blue Lagoon beach (in the Coloured section, of course). Mother and Father would bring a radio as Thurn, Tania, and I would make sand castles and swim, which we learned to do while still toddlers. Father would hold us in his arms as we paddled and splashed, churning the water with furious beats of our legs. Like Father, I was always drawn to the shore and the gentle tug of a slack tide or the roar of high tide in storm season. I would drift on my back, floaties on, bobbing near the shore, the warmth of the water enveloping me, gazing up at wispy clouds above me until I felt like I had disappeared to another world entirely.

Now, in iFafa, I could use the ocean to disappear.

The front yard of the farmhouse faced the Indian Ocean. Although I was not allowed to walk the mile or so to the beach, I could see the water. Nothing else in iFafa shone like the ocean under the African sun. There was a rock at the edge of the farm that was the perfect place to view her. After school, I'd drop my satchel in the front yard, kick off my black shoes and white socks covered in brown dust, and run to the rock. I'd sit there, my toes digging furrows into the African dirt, and imagine I could hear the sound of the distant ocean. In all the empty space between iFafa and the sea, it might have been easy to lose hope, but I could always hear her song. One morning, I woke up before dawn, crept out of the house, and walked the mile to the beach in the dark. I wanted to see the sunrise over the ocean. It took me less time than I had thought, so there was time to stand in the water and enjoy the feel of the sand and the surf brush my feet. Someone else must have had the same idea that morning because as the yellow sun rose over glistening water, I heard music playing from the open windows of a car parked behind me. I would recognize the song years later as "Here Comes the Sun" by the Beatles. Watching the sunrise as the music swelled behind me, the moment coalesced into something more beautiful than any of Father's paintings.

Nearly two decades later, in America, I would stand on another eastern shore over 8,000 miles away. I would listen to the dance of the Atlantic. It was the same. Her name and borders might be different, but she murmured the same living rhythm she had sung to me in iFafa a lifetime before. She beckoned me to join her, so I did. She baptized my feet. I moved further into her waters. She baptized my calves, my thighs. Her currents caressed my body. I fixed my eyes on the smudged sky and watched torn clouds chase each other toward the horizon. I closed my eyes and moved further in. She encircled me. She ran her fingers through my unruly, kinky hair. I felt myself lifted into her embrace, and she held me, cradled in her arms until I allowed myself to let out every tear the world had never seen.

8

SATURDAY BREAKFAST AT IFAFA WAS ALWAYS extra special: fried eggs, bacon, sliced tomatoes, canned beans in tomato sauce, and buttered brown bread. This was our weekend treat as Monday through

Friday Mrs. Fayes served mielie pap with a dollop of butter, a spoonful of sugar and a splash of milk. Though I enjoyed my mielie pap before school, weekend breakfasts were most delicious.

Every Saturday, Tania and I fed the pigs and chickens, collected eggs from the coop, and then made our beds. On days when there were no thunderstorms to shelter from or mushrooms to collect for frying, we were free to play outside after our chores.

It was on just such a Saturday that Tania and I were playing tag on the front yard of the farmhouse. We had begun with a game of hide-and-seek, but when it was my turn to hide, I found a bush that hid me so perfectly Tania passed me three times without seeing me. I was as comfortable as a pig in mud behind that bush, and I could have stayed there for hours, but when she couldn't find me, Tania began to cry, so I came out of hiding, and we switched to a game of tag. Tania was a faster runner than me, so she preferred tag.

And this is how it came to be that Tania and I were playing tag when Mummy came back.

THE BRIGHT IFAFA SKY STRETCHES ABOVE US AS WE run around bushes and fence posts. I am so close to catching Tania my hand brushes against her hair. I resist the urge to grab it. My hiding bush is coming up, and I know Tania will swerve to put it between us, but this time I am ready. I pivot right just as she does, and for a few seconds, we are running parallel to each other. I reach out my arm and easily tag her shoulder. She laughs, and I know freedom will be fleeting. I take off at a run.

I'm scanning the yard for options as I run when I notice a plume of dust in the distance. I stop abruptly. Tania is on me immediately and tags my shoulder. When I don't move to run, she stops and follows my gaze. The plume of dust moves up the road toward us until it coalesces into a car.

We never receive visitors in iFafa, so the sight of this car making its way up the long dirt driveway, kicking up dust, is in itself cause for excitement. I can see that the car is a dull silver and holds a driver and a passenger, but I can't see who they are. I squint, and as the car comes closer, I see a woman sitting in the passenger seat. She has a V-shaped chin just like Mummy. But of course, it can't be. I wonder if my eyes are seeing right.

Then, as the car emerges from the dust kicked up by its wheels and makes its way up the driveway, the face of the woman becomes clear through the windshield. She has eyebrows plucked into thin black lines, and her smooth hair, the color of black ink, catches the iFafa sun and shines through the car window.

Here she is—a most unexpected visit and one I have long awaited. I don't have to go look for her one day, as I'd imagined I would; instead, she comes to me in a dull silver car driven by a man I have never seen before.

FOR SOME REASON, I REMEMBER TANIA AND ME running with our arms flung wide open to greet Mummy, but running with arms flung out is how girls trip and fall, and neither Tania nor I were careless runners, so I suspect this detail is less a memory of what we did but one of how we felt. However we ran, by the time we reached the dull silver car, it had parked outside the house and Mummy had stepped out of the car. Tania and I wrapped her in our arms, and I put my head against her chest and breathed in the familiar aerosol perfume of my fragrant yellow flower.

Her perfume smelled like a thousand wishes come true.

Mummy had returned, but when I looked up at her face, I didn't recognize her.

She had the same smooth olive skin that never burned in the sun but turned a deep, caramel brown. She had the same eyebrows, plucked to wispy lines she filled in softly with pencil, but there was something different about her eyes. Her brown eyes were bright, but when she looked at us, it was as if she were looking past us.

The man Mummy had come with pulled on her and said to Tania and me, "Move out the way. Let me help your mother." He was tall but not as tall as Father. He was dark-skinned with short, thick wavy black hair, a stubby wide nose, and a mustache. He had what is often termed a boxer's physique. Some might have found it attractive, but to my eight-year-old eyes, the effect was wholly intimidating.

Tania and I watched the man wrap his arm around Mummy's waist and drape her arm across his shoulder. They walked away from us, toward the house, and my heart, so full a moment ago, slowly deflated and settled into a puddle at my feet.

IN THE LIVING ROOM, I HIDE BEHIND A CHAIR TO avoid the company of these strangers. I watch as two cups of coffee are quickly prepared and served to each of them. I watch Mummy struggle to hold her cup without spilling. The man next to her catches me staring and shoots me a squinty, fixed glare threatening danger. A sudden chill runs up my spine. I have wished so long for Mummy's return, but it has all come out wrong. I suppose I could have been clearer about my wish. Maybe in between all the sparkles and rainbows, I should have said, "and have her not come back with a man please, especially not a scary-looking one." My Sunday school teachers say nobody should judge another person, but there is no kindness in this man's dark eyes. Surely God knows what I can see so clearly and will not judge me. The man reminds me of the devil himself, though I have no yardstick to measure this by. I have certainly never met the devil before, but nor have I ever met anyone like this man. There is something uncomfortable about the way he looks at others. I don't feel safe looking into his eyes. They make me feel like I have done something wrong.

Mummy calls him "Marcel."

Mummy and Marcel get back in the dull silver car and drive away.

One week, maybe two, and they return. This time, I don't run to Mummy.

Our bags are packed again. We are leaving iFafa. We are leaving with Mummy and the man she calls Marcel. Tania and I are told we will be going to live with Mummy, and Mummy now lived with him.

MR. AND MRS. FAYES STOOD IN THEIR FRONT YARD and waved goodbye to us, and I pressed my hand to the back window as we drove away. It was not so much a goodbye to them as it was a farewell to the distant waters that brought me comfort during my time at their farm. In reality, I never came to know these people with whom we lived for two years. I looked on, past their waving hands, and gazed once more at the distant sea.

We picked up Thurn, and he squeezed into the back seat with us. The car headed down the long dirt road, and the iFafa air turned to a fine, dry powder. Dust floated in a brown mist above the green sugarcane stalks that could have hidden even Father. I had come to take comfort in iFafa's soft, familiar washes of blue, green, and brown. Inside the car, it was a mixture of grey and black, and the air did not smell like the sea or sugarcane, but of sweat and cigarette smoke because Marcel kept the windows up to keep out the dust.

I felt an edge of nervousness, thinking about this new life we were driving toward. I wanted to be back home, but I can't say where home was anymore.

MUMMY SAYS, "I HAVE SOME GOOD NEWS TO SHARE."

Her voice is flat, and Thurn and Tania and I say nothing. No one asks, "What is it, Mummy? Tell us, tell us!"

She continues, "Marcel and I are going to be getting married."

As dust roads turned to gravel, the stones crunched under the weight of Marcel's car.

"So you are going to have a new father," she says; her voice pitches slightly higher on "father."

I watch the sweet cane fields blur past. Unpleasant announcements in cars no longer surprise me.

"What should we call you?" Tania asks the man with Mummy.

"You can call me Dad. Or Marcel."

I listen but don't turn my head from the window.

"Gillian, you're quiet back there," Marcel says. "What do you think of me being your father?"

He looks at me through the rearview mirror and smiles a crooked smile. I don't trust him, but I know better than to give an honest answer.

Smiling politely, I say, "It's nice, thank you."

The man who is not my father looks back at the road, and I look back out the window. The sky is white, but I can't see the sun. "*My mother, but not my Marcel. My mother but not my Marcel.*" Just outside the window, rows of sugarcane whip past. "*Not, mine, not mine, not mine . . .*"

Greenwood Park

9

OVER FIVE HUNDRED YEARS AGO, THE PORTU-
guese explorer, Vasco Da Gama, searching for
a route from Europe to India, passed the east coast
of Africa on Christmas day. He named the land *Natal*,
"Christmas" in Portuguese, and sailed on. Three hundred
and twenty-seven years later, the British, hoping to open
trade relations with the monarch of the Zulu kingdom,
Shaka kaSenzangakhona, or Shaka Zulu, established a
trading post on the east coast of Africa and called it Port
Natal. On the north shores of Port Natal, a capital city
was built and named for the British general and colonial administrator, Sir Benjamin D'Urban. Under the
Apartheid system, Durban, with Natal Province, would
be divided into increasingly segregated neighborhoods.

In 1980, Granny, together with my uncle Nicki, her
youngest surviving child, would search the Coloured
neighborhoods of the coastal town of Durban for a
house for Mummy and Mummy's new husband. After
iFafa, we lived in an outbuilding in a poor Indian area

of Durban, and Granny and Uncle Nicki felt our new family needed a stable place to live.

They found Greenwood Park, a community carved out of subtropical thicket with certain sections for Coloureds and others for Indians. Following the asphalt scars that wound up the steep slopes of Durban, they found a house which sat at the bend of a road, flanked by weary palms.

Granny and Uncle Nicki purchased the house in Greenwood Park and, with it, peace of mind knowing that Thurn, Tania, and I now had a mother, a father, and a decent house to live in. Thurn was ten, I was nine, Tania was eight, and for the first time in over six years, we had a home address: 19 Sentinel Avenue, Greenwood Park, Durban, Natal Province, South Africa.

19 Sentinel Avenue, with its triangular tin roof and patchy yard bordered by cinder blocks, was humble by American standards, but Thurn, Tania, and I goggled at its three bedrooms, two bathrooms, electricity, hot water, veranda, television, and telephone. The floors of the house were hardwood, standard in older homes in South Africa, except for one, in the back of the house. This became the bedroom Tania and I would share, and for reasons unknown to me, it was carpeted a faded red that struck me as both ugly and incomprehensible.

Ostensibly, Thurn had his own room—a long, narrow one—but it also served as a weight room where Marcel kept his dumbbells and exercise bench. Marcel worked out regularly and was quite arrogant about his appearance, frequently strutting around the house shirtless.

I was eight years old when Mummy married Marcel. This was when the nightmares began.

HE NEVER SITS ON OUR BED THE WAY FATHER DID. There is no comfort. No affection. I feel his hands in the dark and in the shadows and the rustle of the night. My body is stiff with fear. Through the fog of sleep, there is a sense of falling, and my hands reach out to him. I need help, even from him, from anyone who can wake me. I want to scream, but my voice, like the lights, is shut off. He leans heavy into me. I fight to breathe. Is it the covers I wrap tightly around my body each night that make it difficult to breathe? Then he breathes for both of us, and the warm, muggy breath jolts me back to the room I share with Tania.

Words finally come: "What are you doing?"

Silence.

He slips out the door like mist and is gone before I can be sure if what just happened was real or imagined. I turn to Tania. She is sound asleep as the world ticks forward. My heart knocks against my chest long after I have awoken. I rearrange the blankets and wrap them even tighter around my boiling body. Exhaustion eventually takes over, and I fall back to sleep.

This nightmare repeats night after night after night.

GRANNY HAS AGREED TO WATCH TANIA, THURN, and I one evening, while Mummy and Marcel go out with friends. They assure Granny they will return very early the next morning to pick us up for a beach outing. I can hardly sleep that night, too excited at the prospect of going to the ocean, my favorite place. I toss and turn, imagining swimming in those sparkling waters and listening to sounds of crashing waves. The sounds of the ocean are as much music to my ears as the sound of Uncle Johnny's guitar is to Granny.

"Come, you children must get up," Granny says, shaking us awake. "They are going to fetch you soon." Granny is very organized and has everything packed for us since the night before: blankets, towels, changes of clothes for each of us, sandwiches, and Oros orange juice. It is five o'clock in the morning, and the second time Granny has woken us up with sandwiches and Oros orange juice. I bounce out of bed the moment I hear her voice. We all dress quickly, then gulp down our hot tea before scurrying to the front door to wait. The air hums with expectancy as we await the sound of the car rumbling down the driveway. We watch the clock on the wall change from five to six, then to seven, eight, nine, ten.

With each passing hour, our excitement deflates, replaced by disappointment. It is late morning when Mummy and Marcel finally drive up. They are both drunk. Granny is beside herself, and neither Mummy nor Marcel makes their way through her door that day. Granny scolds them like schoolchildren, so fiercely her false teeth fly out of her mouth.

IT WAS IN THIS COLOURED HOUSE, IN A COLOURED community, of Apartheid South Africa where Mummy met Richelieu. Richelieu called on her regularly, whispering to her his warm, amber-colored promises of full-bodied escape. Monday through Thursday she wouldn't touch a drop of liquor, but come Fridays, Saturdays, and all holidays, Mummy drank these promises straight from a 750ml bottle. Marcel would watch her stagger through the kitchen or slump on the couch. "Look at you, you drunk!" he would yell, his mouth curled with disdain. "You disgust me." If he caught any of us children looking at him, he would shout, "What the hell are you looking at? Get to your bladdy rooms, you rubbishes, before I get my belt out!" Tania and I always did as instructed, bolting to our room where we didn't dare so much as sneeze. In our bedroom, we could hear Mummy crying out in the living room, a wrenching howl after each verbal, and sometimes physical, lashing Marcel inflicted on her. When the yelling stopped, I would quietly tiptoe out to check on Mummy.

Mummy had a grip on me like quicksand: soft and enveloping, yet inescapable and lethal. I yearned to be freed of the confines of the house, but I was sucked into Mummy's hopelessness. She was my one remaining parent, and it terrified me to witness her in this crippled state. I didn't feel unbridled love for her—it was mixed with contempt and pity—but I knew I could not lose my only parent left in this world, damaged or not. I needed to protect her, and so I carried her pain along with mine.

On the nights when she was unable to reach her bed, I would carry a blanket and pillow to her. I would gently place her head atop the pillow and cover her limp body with the blanket.

I AM NINE YEARS OLD. IT IS ONE OF THE FEW TIMES Marcel's omnipresent shadow does not blanket the house; he has gone somewhere overnight, and I do not care one whit. It is the only time I can recall ever sleeping in Mummy's bed. Tania and I are both in the bed, and for once, we are the family I wish we could be.

I wake from sleep and into silence. No clock ticks, no floor squeaks, no wind whispers at the window or tugs at the eaves. Whether a tap on my shoulder or a feeling of being watched, I cannot say, but I have been gently awakened.

I open my eyes and look to the side of the bed. There is nobody there. To the right of me, Tania sleeps silently, and to her right, Mummy is peacefully and solidly asleep. A movement from the corner of my eye catches my attention. I sit up in the bed to see what it might be.

From Mummy's bedroom, I have a clear view of the family room. There, in the corner, are two shapes, wispy and white and flowing like veils. They dance slowly, soundlessly. I can't distinguish facial features, but I notice their hair. It flows with them as they dance, and I have the sense they are smiling.

Their dancing slows, they linger there in the corner, hovering, and beckon me with what looks like hands. I rub the smudge of sleep from my eyes, and when I open again, the white figures are still there and have resumed their dance. I see their invisible smiles, and I smile back at them. I am not afraid in the least.

For some reason, I know they are a mother and daughter. I don't know how I know this; I just do. They beckon me again to join in their dance. I don't leave the bed. I don't want to disrupt the moment.

I rub my eyes a second time, thinking they will disappear. They remain. Their dance continues, like reflected light off water, swaying back and forth before me. They watch me, too.

I lean back on my pillow, wondering who they might be, where they have come from. It feels as if they know me. Eventually, they fade slowly into the night, and when I can no longer see them, I put my arm over Tania. The night is peaceful, and I fall asleep.

I never tell a single soul what I saw, and I never see them again.

AS OFTEN AS HE TURNED ON MY MOTHER, MARCEL turned on Thurn even more. Thurn was not a trouble-maker, really. None of us were. We listened and took orders very well, but Marcel would always find, or manufacture, a reason to physically punish each of us. If the dog wasn't fed on time (though there was no specific time we knew of), Thurn would be summoned for a whipping, delivered using Marcel's favorite thick belt. If school shoes weren't polished to Marcel's liking, the snapping of his belt rang through the house, summoning Thurn to go to his room. Tania and I got a bamboo stick when it was our turn, but Thurn bore the brunt of the beatings. It was extraordinarily painful for me to hear his cries echoing through the house as he received his lashes, all the while begging Marcel for mercy.

If there was consistency in our house, this was it. This was the broken record that played every weekend.

MUMMY IS COOKING IN THE KITCHEN, AND MARCEL walks by. As usual, he is shirtless, and as he passes, she throws salt over her shoulder. I have often seen her throw salt over her shoulder when Marcel walks past her—she says she is warding off the evil walking inside the house—but on this day, he catches her doing it. I don't think he actually sees her since his back is to her, but he must have felt the grains land on his bare skin.

He turns on her. "What the hell do you think you're doing throwing salt at me? What do you think I am?"

Mummy is silent.

"I'm talking to you!" he screams. "Answer me!"

"I just put too much salt in the food and threw the rest away," Mummy says.

I think this is a good answer, but it doesn't work for Marcel.

He turns to us children, who are quivering as we watch. "I'm sick of all of you!" he yells. "Get to your rooms!"

Thurn, Tania and I run to our bedrooms at the back of the house, but I can still hear Mummy's cries as Marcel beats her and calls her names I can't repeat.

IN PHYSICS, ONE WAY TO CATEGORIZE WAVES IS BY the direction the individual particles move relative to the direction the wave moves. When the individual particles of the medium move parallel to the direction the wave moves, this is called a longitudinal wave. Sound traveling through air is this type of wave.

Sound waves travel at 767.291 miles per hour. The volume and intensity of sound—be it music, a whisper, a scream—is measured in decibels. The threshold for causing damage to the human ear is approximately 135 decibels sustained over half an hour. The reflections of sound waves moving within a room, a hall, or another enclosed space are called reverberations. A scientist may tell you differently, but the sound of a belt striking skin and accompanied by a child's cry of pain moves nowhere near the speed of sound; it is far slower, and the reverberations live with a person for years.

Thirty years on, and I hear them still.

Sometimes I would hear Mummy pray during Thurn's beatings: "Dear God, please help me. Save my children and me from this. I can't take it. Make him stop." Between prayers, Mummy would go into the kitchen to swig from a glass of brandy she kept hidden in the cupboard, smoke a cigarette, and cry. Then she would return to her prayers. If the sounds of the beatings continued to reverberate throughout the house, she would get out her little plastic bottle filled with holy water from St. Michael's Church and sprinkle it around the house. Then, another swig of brandy.

Many nights, she wasn't able to make it to her room before her legs crumpled beneath her in the living room or hallway. The first time I saw her lying on the living room floor, unable to pick herself up, I panicked. "Mummy, what's wrong? Please, please get up!" I begged. "Are you okay?"

"Isperfetallyfine," she slurred. "Ishorry, nuffink you-cando." Barely intelligible words stumbled from her mouth, while tears trickled down her face like ripples in quiet water, then the words turned to sobs, the kind of gut-wrenching wails that accompany the exposure of deep-rooted pain. I watched her misery with helpless fear and uncertainty.

Mummy spent weekends in periodic bouts of destructive drinking and weekdays working in town selling women's clothing. In the evenings, she saw to a clean house and well-cooked meals.

One of my favorite dishes of Mummy's was lamb *biryani*, a traditional Indian dish of layered rice, lentils, and meat, adopted by Coloureds and Whites alike; because of the country's varied population, South African cuisine is diverse with a strong Indian influence. Mummy was liberal with spices as she cooked her biryani, and the house would fill with a heavenly fragrance. I liked to watch her in the kitchen as she diced onions and tomatoes, then sautéed them with curry powder, chili powder, garlic, and salt. And this was just the start: still to come were the fresh curry leaves, bay leaves, and cilantro. It took Mummy hours to prepare this dish, and she paid careful attention to its creation on Sundays.

Those delicious meals, however, lasted only as long as Mummy and Marcel's paycheck. Payday was the last Friday of each month, and neither Mummy nor Marcel managed their finances well. Payday would come, and Mummy would buy thirty days of groceries the same day. Without fail, by the end of each month and days before payday, we were faced with empty cupboards.

On special occasions and occasional Sundays, Granny would bring over one or two live chickens for dinner and her bush knife. We referred to this meal as "running fowl."

First, Granny would use her bush knife to chop off the heads of the live chickens, letting their bodies drop to the ground. The chickens would run around the yard, blood spewing from their necks. When the chickens finally collapsed, Granny would dip them into boiling water, then pluck their feathers and clean them before cooking. The sight of the blood and the smell of freshly killed chickens being plunged into boiling water would make me sick with nausea. "Running fowl" was not a favorite of mine as it was for Mummy. Mummy loved running fowl.

IT'S SUNDAY, A WEEK BEFORE PAYDAY, AND THERE is nothing but a single chicken and a couple of potatoes left. When the chicken is cooked and served for lunch, I eat my portion of chicken as though it is my last meal, sucking the marrow from the bones until there is nothing left to eat. By evening, our stomachs are rumbling, and I worry what we will eat the rest of the week.

"Go over to Granny's and ask if you can borrow some bread, onions, tomatoes, and a can of corn, Gillian," Mummy says.

The walk to Granny's house is no more than two miles, but knowing I am on my way to borrow food makes it feel much longer. I know Granny will not be happy and I will be the one who has to listen to her grumble.

"*Ag,* why is your mother so irresponsible?" Granny says. It is more of a statement than a question. "You know, I don't have much money, but I don't let these sorts of things happen. She is bladdy lucky you are asking, or I would say no. I know how much you like corn, Gillian. Otherwise, your mother and Marcel can just bugger off."

IT'S THE LAST FRIDAY OF THE MONTH, AND THURN, Tania, and I wait eagerly for the empty cupboards to be filled. We roam the house hungrily, anticipating the evening arrival of groceries. End-of-the-month Friday dinners are always a feast, and tonight we dine on fried steak and onions, eggs, and fresh bread smothered with butter. Lying in bed with our bellies full, I turn to Tania, "You know, White people eat this way all the time." She responds: "It must be really nice to be White."

10

THE HOUSE GRANNY AND UNCLE NICKI BOUGHT for us on Sentinel Avenue had a giant mango tree in the side yard. This tree became my private playground, where I could climb as I dared, and no one could find me. From up high, I could see all the neighborhood houses below and the plants and trees surrounding them. I imagine Greenwood Park got its name because of the lush greenery that filled the neighborhood, greenery that must have been appealing to the Whites who once lived there, but they had moved on to even greener pastures in Durban North, to neighborhoods with ocean views. As Mummy would say, "Must be nice to be White. You get the best jobs, the best houses, and the best views."

In the back yard was a small one-bedroom outbuilding where our African maid lived. This was not because we were wealthy. This was because we were Coloured. Whites asserted their superiority over us by limiting employment opportunities. In turn, we could assert our superiority by employing Africans as domestic help. And such help was inexpensive.

In South Africa at the time, it was not uncommon for Coloured and Indian families to have yard boys and maids. Our maid's name was Maude. She did housework during the week and went to her homeland on weekends to visit family. In the outbuilding where she stayed, was an old twin size steel bed perched on bricks. I asked Maude one day about why her bed was raised on bricks, and she told me about the *Tokoloshe,* an evil dwarf-like water spirit who caused illness and even killed people. She said he especially liked to harm children and would leave scratches on their bodies. She said the Tokoloshe could even become invisible and live in your body, which is why she kept her bed on bricks; in this way, he could not reach her while she slept.

I didn't know anything about Tokoloshes, but I knew bedrooms were the worst places for keeping safe. I preferred to be outdoors, especially during the day when Mummy and Marcel weren't around. There was no one to fear, no drunkenness to contend with; I was only responsible for myself. So I did cartwheels on the grass, played hopscotch with Tania, told stories with friends, read poetry (in secret, because Marcel would not have approved), made mud cakes, or played games like cops and robbers or cowboys and Indians with bows and arrows we made ourselves. The arrows were bamboo sticks sharpened to the point of a fine pencil which we would shoot at each other with bows also made of bamboo, bent and tied with fishing line we passed through small holes at either end. One day when a shot arrow landed in the middle of my right eye, I started bleeding. Fortunately, there was no permanent damage, but I felt considerably less safe playing cops and robbers after that. In the mango tree, I felt safe. No one could touch me there.

"Girls don't climb trees," Granny would say to Tania and me. "It's fine for a boy to have scraped knees and legs, but not for a girl. A girl becomes a lady, and how do you think it will look if you march around town with broken bones and scarred legs? *Ag, man,* I'm telling you, if you do, the only person who will want to marry you is a kaffir, and you don't want that." Mummy never objected to us climbing trees, and Marcel didn't give a bugger-all, so I spent a lot of time in my mango tree.

The mango tree stood tall, its deep roots firmly planted in the African soil. I loved that tree, with its umbrella of deep green, glossy leaves. When temperatures reached unbearable highs, as they frequently did in the African summer months, there was shelter to be found in its shade. I watched the tree with careful eyes each year as the buds turned into flowers, then formed tiny green mangos, and finally flourished into ripe golden fruits. I would eat these mangoes to the point where my stomach could take no more, then with a satisfied smile, I would fling the pips in the air and watch them land below me. To this day, they are the sweetest mangos I've ever tasted.

Under the tree was a chair that must have been as old as the house. Its metal frame was rusted, and only two wooden planks remained of its seat. When we lived in Sydenham, Father would take perfectly good wood and bury it in the dirt for some time. After the white ants had eaten away at it, he would paint the wood and make frames from it. He said he liked the organic look of the wood after it was dug up. The planks of the old chair under the mango tree looked like wood Father would have used to make frames.

During school breaks when Tania, Thurn, and neighborhood friends went inside to watch television, I went to the tree. It always puzzled me as to why everyone liked being indoors watching television, especially when there was so much to do outside, and television choices were so paltry. Programs only came on in the late afternoon, and there were only three channels to choose from, all controlled by the government. Of the three channels, I would have only considered watching the English language one, since the other two were in Afrikaans, a language I hated. A Dutch tongue in origin, Afrikaans was the language of the Whites, and they didn't like us, so why should I like their language? It was a required subject in school, so I learned just enough to get by, but I never spoke it if given a choice. I knew the same could be argued of English, but my communication options were limited. Either way, English or Afrikaans, I preferred to be outside, especially up in my mango tree. Though I climbed high up above the ground, I wasn't ever scared. The branches were thick, and they kept me safe.

IT'S BEEN RAINING, AND WHEN THE RAIN STOPS, Thurn and I make a bet. Hanging from the very top of the tree is a huge mango we have both been eyeing.

Thurn says, "I bet I can get that mango before you can."

"No you can't. I'm a fast climber."

"No you're not. Boys are faster than girls."

"That's stupid."

"Well, prove it, then."

"Fine."

We are both standing at the base of the tree. Thurn says, "Okay, I'll say 'on your mark, get set, go!' Only then can we start climbing."

"Okay, but first swear on your life you won't cheat."

"Who said I'm going to cheat?"

"Nobody. It's just a good thing to do before a bet."

"Whatever."

Thurn heads toward the tree.

"Wait," I say. "You're taller than me. I have to use the chair; otherwise, I won't be able to get into the tree."

"That's cheating."

"No it's not."

"Well, if you use the chair, then we start the race when we're both in the tree."

"All right."

I step up onto the seat of the chair and grab hold of a branch to pull myself up. The bark of the tree is still slick with rain, and I push against the chair to help me up. Finally, my hands get a grip on the branch, and I scramble into the tree. The chair falls away from under my feet. I look down to see the rustic chair, glazed with rainwater, lying on the green grass. Suddenly, Thurn pushes his way in front of me and has already taken the lead.

"Hey, we were supposed to start at the same time!"

Thurn doesn't hear me or pretends not to.

I eye the shiny prize waiting for me and begin to climb. My senses are alive, and I hardly notice the hairy worms crawling on the tree's branches. I don't like these worms because they sting, though not in the same way as a bee. When you touch the hair on these caterpillars, their spines break away and release toxins, which sting your skin, but I'm too much in a hurry to be concerned about them today.

Just before I reach the top, I feel my leg slip on a wet branch. One moment I am rushing forward, and the next I'm falling through the branches. Everything slows. I look up and see Thurn's shocked face staring down at me. I feel the rush of air on my dirt worn skin. I know pain is coming. I close my eyes. My body twists, and I hit the ground. I land face-down in the dirt, but my left leg is elevated and has a rusty iron poking halfway through it. I can't feel anything, but I start to scream. My wailing attracts the attention of Maude, who rushes to my side and starts doing what looks like a Zulu dance but not a happy one. She is clapping her hands with panic and covering her mouth and saying, "*Hayibo, hayibo, hayibo!*" and jumping all around me. I yell, "Maude, please take it out!"

But she is scared and wears a look like she just wants to run back to the homelands. I think all the blood pouring from my leg has sent her into a frenzy. Maybe she thinks the Tokoloshe is to blame and wants nothing to do with it. Zulu people are very superstitious.

She calls the neighbor's yard boy, Lucky, to come over, and when he comes running, she tells him, "The child is pissing blood by the leg." Lucky is not fazed. He approaches me and—sharp and quick thinking as ever—yanks the iron rod out. Lucky isn't really a boy but a man. I've caught myself studying him when I'm sitting in the safety of the mango tree. I've guessed he is in his early twenties. He is not slow-moving and can whip a yard into shape in no time.

I can see now why Maude is so upset. There is a gaping hole in my leg, with white flesh sticking out and bright red blood flowing from it. She tosses me an old towel and points. "Put this round the leg."

I wait a few hours for Mummy to return from work. When she does, Granny and Uncle Johnny are with her, and I am taken to the doctor, who tells me it is too late for stitches and to expect a permanent scar. He cleans the wound and patches me up with a bandage. When it heals, the skin forms a perfect triangle-shaped scar, like the roof of our house. I'm sure Granny isn't happy with me—this certainly diminishes my marriage prospects.

MARCEL HAD AN EYE FOR SPOTTING WEAKNESSES in people and was either quick to exploit them or patient in waiting for the opportune time to do so. For Marcel, weaknesses were the perfect breeding ground for fear.

While Marcel exercised in Thurn's room, he would call us in separately. Thurn was always first, me second, and Tania last. When it was my turn, I would walk in as if I were walking through Hell's gates, trying to hide my nervousness as best I could. My weakness was math. Not losing the rhythm of his weightlifting, Marcel would bark out an order: "Sit down and tell me what is 9×9!" and I would nervously count on my fingers, hidden as I sat on my hands. If he caught me, he would yell, "Put your hands out!" After I obeyed, my hands trembling in front of me, he would put his weights down to grab the bamboo stick, holding it up high above his head before bringing it down hard on my palms. "If you count on your hands, you'll get another one of these." Even if I knew my multiplication, my mind went blank the moment I walked into the room. All my focus was always on the stick. After three or four lashings, I would be ordered out of the room.

"Get out of here! And tomorrow, you had better know your division."

Once, when I wasn't able to come up with the right answer, he became so angry he dropped the stick and took off one of his shoes and threw it at me. "You're so damned stupid!"

As much as I hated Marcel, I loved Uncle Nicki, Mummy's youngest sibling. He called me "my tail" because I followed him everywhere, just like I did with Father. Even though I was young, Nicki captivated me with his profound passion for righting the wrongs we had been exposed to in South Africa, which he called "Azania."

Though I loved being around Nicki, I didn't see him often. He lived in Johannesburg, and so our interactions were limited to holidays and occasional telephone calls. On one such phone conversation when I was ten years old, I asked him if he would teach me a new word every time we spoke. I wanted an extensive vocabulary just like him. The possibility thrilled me. He agreed.

"Okay, Gillian, your first word shall be *sophisticated*," Nicki said. He then gave me the definition and encouraged me to practice the word as much as I could in everyday conversation until we spoke again, at which time he would teach me a new word. It was as if I had been given a beautiful new dress. I was so eager to try this new word and show it off to everyone that I got off the phone and immediately began using it. Lavishly.

"Mummy, you have a very sophisticated look today."

"Tania, you sound very sophisticated."

And on I went.

Until Marcel put an unsophisticated end to it all.

"The next time I hear you use that word, I will beat you so bladdy hard you won't know what hit you. You think you're somebody, but you're not. You won't ever amount to anything, so don't bother trying. You hear me?"

"Yes."

"Yes, who?"

"Yes, Marcel."

"Now get out of my sight!"

My teachers weren't much different from Marcel, and frequently used rulers and bamboo sticks as a form of punishment when I didn't have a ready answer. Imagine my surprise when I was one of three students selected to participate in a speech and debate competition. More than surprised—confused. I had been chosen along with Andrea and Luis, the two smartest students at our school. Andrea's father was a doctor, and Luis, though he lived with his grandparents just down the road, was nothing like me.

I had no idea how I ended up in their company. Andrea and Luis cared about doing well in school. I'd stopped trying hard at anything except for the egg and spoon race on sports day. I used to be in Class A but was now in Class B, the class for those with middling academic ability at Greenwood Park Primary. I liked being in Class B because nobody paid much attention to us. Class A was filled with all the smart students, and the teachers were always praising them; Class C also got talked about a lot, as those students usually ended up in the principal's office. Many C class students failed to pass their classes and had to repeat their standards. One of the most beloved teachers at Greenwood Park, Mr. Africa, once joked, "Yoh! When I first got to Greenwood Park, I was made the Standard 5C class teacher, and most of those students were almost as old and big as me." Mr. Africa would later negotiate with Mr. Clarivette, the principal, to end the labeling of children by their academic abilities and have classes named according to the teacher's surname.

Being in the B class was like being the middle child, and I was comfortable there. Teachers didn't expect us to be high achievers, so they were more easy-going, but they also didn't expect us to ditch class by lunchtime, so they gave us just the right amount of discipline. As a B student, it was easy to get by without attracting much attention.

But this competition had pulled me out of my complacent oblivion and into the spotlight.

I shared the news with Mummy. She said Father would be so proud of me. Marcel grunted and walked away.

We practiced with Mrs. Winter after school, and she asked us all sorts of questions on a variety of subjects. When we didn't know the answer, she gave us tips on how to answer appropriately anyway. Mostly, she said how impressed she was with us. She also told us we would be competing with students from White schools, so we would need to be at our sharpest and represent Greenwood Park Primary School to the best of our abilities.

Mrs. Winter knew she did not have to worry too much: Andrea and Luis were bookworms, and not only smart but also very well-mannered. And while I was no shining light, I always did exactly as I was told. I suppose it also helped that I had a good memory.

ON THE NIGHT OF THE COMPETITION, MRS. WINTER picks each of us up and drives us to a White school in Durban. We are nervous, but we look very sharp in our freshly pressed uniforms, polished shoes, and crisp blazers. Andrea and I both have our hair plaited, with green ribbons tied to the ends.

Inside the school, however, my sharp look begins to dull. I'm not used to wearing a blazer; it's heavy, and I'm sweating all over. The place is filled. White people sit on one side of the room, and us Coloureds sit on the opposite side. The Whites look at us and smirk.

"Don't let them get under your skin," Mrs. Winter says. "Stay focused. Remember all I have taught you. You children are just as smart as them."

The blazer is really bothering me.

Various schools from the Durban area are represented at the competition with teams of White students going up against teams of Coloured students. We watch and listen as the Coloured teams who go before us are given a lambasting. The topics don't seem fair or appropriate for our level, and it becomes apparent this "competition" is more of a public show.

I'm really sweating now, but I try to remain hopeful in the face of Mrs. Winter's encouragement. Plus, I remind myself, two of Greenwood Park's smartest students are here with me.

Then it's our turn to go up on stage. The lights are bright. The blazer itches at my skin like chickenpox, but I don't scratch. I stand proud.

The moderator asks us something about "space," but honestly, his words are so big I would be beaten up for even thinking them. We try our best, stumbling through our delivery, but one question and several minutes of verbal fumbling later, we walk off stage, heads down, humiliated, ultimately lambasted like our fellow Coloured peers.

I have never seen Mrs. Winter upset. She has a calm disposition, and she never yells at students like the other teachers do. Because of this, she is a favorite of mine as much as Mr. Africa. On that night, she becomes my favorite teacher even more. She does not reprimand us for embarrassing Greenwood Park Primary. With a clenched jaw and narrowed eyes, she lashes out, not at us, but at the injustice of it all.

"We will never again accept such an invitation," she says. "Trust me. Tonight had nothing to do with any of you and your intellectual competence. The topics covered were not what they initially informed me, and the questions asked of *our* teams were not age-appropriate. We were set up to fail tonight. To make us think and feel that we are not as smart as the White man. This was Apartheid."

11

ONE DAY, AUNTY VAL DECIDED SHE'D HAD enough of living as a poor Coloured person trying to make ends meet, so she packed up a few things and moved to Jo'burg. She left behind everything indicating she was Coloured—her birth certificate, photos, memorabilia, and other things of that nature—and she made herself "White."

"It will be a brand-new start," she said. "Nobody will know me there, and I'll get a good, White, paying job and make something of myself instead of rotting away in Sydenham and going nowhere fast. Besides, my blimmin options for a husband around here are corner boys and gangsters. To bladdy hell with that!"

Aunty Val was tall, especially for a woman. Taller than all my aunts and uncles, she had fair skin just like Granny and me. She kept her hair cut short and dyed blonde, and her nails were always perfectly filed and polished. She also smoked; the moment one cigarette went out, she would light another. When she smoked, she put a filter on the tip and held it between her long, elegant fingers. She made smoking seem like such a proper thing to do, not like how Mummy smoked, which was in moments of stress. If I had been permitted, I might have gone so far as to say that Aunty Val looked very *sophisticated* when she smoked. Aunty Val's elegance seemed natural, though, in retrospect, it may have been a learned elegance, one she cultivated after many years of "playing White" in Jo'burg. I suppose I will never know.

We liked it when Aunty Val came to visit. She made fancy White people food we hadn't eaten before, like little melon balls rolled in sugar and served in the glass bowls we only got to use on very special occasions like Christmas.

Not everyone was agreeable with Aunty Val playing White. Uncle Nicki thought it shameful that his own sister was rubbing shoulders with the enemy. He also lived in Johannesburg, but in the Coloured section of town. He had returned from Botswana, where he had been living in exile for two years. Nicki's exile had been technically self-imposed, though the fact that he was on the government's hit list left his options limited.

He was a comrade and had long ago joined AZAPO (the Azanian People's Organization), one of the many Black Consciousness groups that had sprouted up across the country, with sister organizations around the world and connections to foreign governments that helped them procure weapons to fight the Apartheid regime. He was involved in the movement at a leadership level, which meant his risk was greater, but which also allowed him to leverage secret channels to eventually make his way back into South Africa. Even then, he mostly kept his distance from us: he was still on the government's hit list after all and didn't want his politics to compromise our safety. The family was worried for him, but there was nothing anyone could say or do. Nicki would never be caught holding a white flag. He was in this fight good and proper, and he loathed the fact that his own sister pretended to be White.

Granny tended to be more sympathetic toward Aunty Val's stance; she was hopeful that marriage would help Nicki "settle down" and abandon his grand thoughts about overthrowing the White government. As it turned out, things only intensified after he and Gabi got married; we would go for long periods without hearing from Nicki, so long that Granny would become convinced he was dead. But, as Nicki often said, "the revolution will not be televised."

When he and Gabi got married in 1981, we went to Johannesburg for the wedding, and Aunty Val didn't show up. She and Nicki got into a huge fight about how despicable it was that she was betraying her oppressed brothers and sisters. Granny tried to mediate. Both Aunty Val and Nicki were staunch in their convictions. Still, I don't know if Aunty Val not showing up had to do with her being afraid that her White friends and colleagues would see her in a Coloured neighborhood, or if Nicki simply did not want a White impersonator at his wedding.

Apartheid created a bitter divisiveness across the country, throughout communities, and within families, just as it was designed to do. Fighting was usually a given at family gatherings, especially after alcohol had been consumed. As Aunty Val frequently said, "a drunk person speaks a sober man's mind."

WE ARE AT OUR HOUSE, AND IT IS EARLY SATURDAY evening. The grown-ups have been drinking all afternoon, and it is turning into a real *jol* with music, food, beers, wine, brandy, and laughing.

"Far as I'm concerned, you need money to be really happy," Uncle Leon says. Uncle Leon must not be happy, because he doesn't have much money. I know this because he is always between jobs and lives in a *pozzy* with rats. He has been staying with us for a little, while he is getting things sorted out, but I am not sure how much sorting he's doing because he likes to hang out with the corner boys, who everyone knows to stay away from.

Mummy says, "*Ja*, I agree, but how can we make good money when the White people have all the good jobs? All the good blimmin jobs go to them!"

"Well, the Coolie who owns the tearoom at the corner has more money than all of us, and he is blimmin miserable," Aunty Myrtle chimes in.

Everyone laughs.

But within minutes, a simmering tension has replaced the laughter, and Aunty Myrtle becomes very cross and begins throwing around accusations.

"You bladdy well think you're better than everyone cause you have fair-skinned children! Well, *voetsek*!"

"Actually, Myrtle, I never said anything about my children, so maybe you better just stop drinking now."

Mummy should not have spoken these words to Aunty Myrtle because now there is real trouble.

Mummy and her sister Myrtle frequently clash, though Aunty Myrtle has arguments with just about everybody in the family. Temperamental and bitter, one word whispered wrong will make her *gatvol*. And if alcohol is involved, which it always is at gatherings, then boy oh boy do the conversations get hectic. Too often, our parties turn into the kind of showdowns I see in those Western movies my school shows us on occasional Fridays after classes, except instead of guns, it's knives. Coloureds can't own guns.

Aunty Myrtle waves her glass in Mummy's direction. I think she might throw it. "Who the fuck do you think you are telling me to stop drinking? You're the one who is bladdy drunk here."

"Look, calm down, Myrtle," Uncle Leon says. He is younger than both Aunty Myrtle and Mummy but older than Nicki, so he likes to take charge. "Nobody's accusing you of anything. It's the system keeping us fighting like this. *Tjoon* me this, when . . ."

"*Ay,* I'm *tjooning* you nothing!" Aunty Myrtle interrupts. "The bladdy system has nothing to do with Lorraine calling me drunk! She deserves a *klap.*"

Granny sees that things are quickly heating up. The grown-ups are starting to get louder and not in a fun way.

"There's no more drinks left, so everyone better go home now," Granny says, standing up to start shutting things down.

"*Ay,* I'm not done here, so somebody better turn some bladdy water into wine before I lose my cool!" Aunty Myrtle says.

With tempers flaring, I know to run for cover, so I climb the mango tree in the side yard. From there, I watch as the aunties and uncles run from the veranda into the front yard. At this point, everyone is fighting each other. It's like a bar fight that starts out between just two people, but within seconds every person in the establishment is involved. I remain hidden in the safety of the tree and watch the unfolding drama from my place of concealment.

Uncle Leon now has a knife in his hand and is threatening Marcel. I feel both terribly scared and thrilled at the idea of Uncle Leon giving Marcel a proper stabbing and teaching him a lesson. Maybe then he will go away and leave us alone.

Everyone else is behaving like they usually do when they have drunk too much:

Mummy is the crying drunk.

Aunty Myrtle is the angry drunk who will bite your head off with her words.

Uncle Leon is the "don't mess with me" drunk who will *moer* someone good and proper and is not afraid to pull out a knife and use it if necessary.

Uncle Johnny tries his best to be the voice of reason, but his voice is drowned out, as it usually is at these things. Even though he is married to Granny, he is not anybody's father, and nobody ever listens to him.

Jupiter, our dog, seems frightened, too. His tail is down between his legs as he stands just below me, at the base of the mango tree. Dogs are usually kept for security purposes and are considered outdoor creatures, so he is never allowed inside. Actually, nobody I know lets their dogs inside, but I hear that White people do. Aunty Val says so.

Unfortunately, Aunty Val isn't here. Her "Whites Only" job with the Chamber of Commerce allows her the luxury of traveling often. She sends us postcards from all the countries she travels to. Uncle Nicki isn't here either. If there are two people in the family I want here, it is them, but instead, I am hiding in the mango tree.

As I tightly hug the branch, the scene below me seems far away, as though it belongs to a different world, like a movie on a screen. Only when Granny's sharp voice rings out am I snapped back into reality: "Everybody get out!" Like a knight without a horse, Granny pulls from God-knows-where her well-used bush knife. It makes the small knife Uncle Leon is holding look like a toy. For a moment, everything comes to a standstill, and then everyone runs for the front gate. Granny sure knows how to clean up a party gone bad.

UNCLE NICKI WAS CONTEMPLATIVE, WELL-READ, deliberate, and articulate. He saw tensions in the Coloured community and in our family for what they were.

"For, in the final analysis, we have lived the experience of being a 'subspecies' in the mind and in the eye of white dominance. If you have not read Frantz Fanon's *Black Skin, White Masks*, I suggest you do," Nicki would say. "It is important we understand the history of the effects of racism and dehumanization inherent in situations of colonial domination on the human psyche." He always said, "to understand where we are going, we must understand where we have been."

Nicki didn't just talk change, however. He was change. Unlike the rest of the family, Nicki rolled up his sleeves and dug right into the dirt to expose the moves and counter moves that drove the engines of Apartheid. Becoming a comrade with AZAPO wasn't some radical, impulsive choice for him. As long as I'd known him, he had never taken the easy path. He was imbued with a sense of purpose and moral conviction, and never deviated from what he held to be true. In 1982, he launched an AZAPO branch in Johannesburg, the Gauteng Branch, and marched forward in his revolutionary struggle for liberation from the Apartheid regime. The branch was big and influential, encompassing a few hundred fellow comrades, and they were part of the "goings-on" Granny complained about.

By 1984, Nicki was giving a speech at the United Nations about the atrocities happening in South Africa under Apartheid. Two higher up leaders of the AZAPO organization had been jailed for their anti-Apartheid activities, and Nicki, next in line, was asked to attend in their place. He did so without hesitation. When he returned to South Africa, the government immediately revoked his passport. He barely made it off the plane before he was stripped of his freedom to travel.

Nicki was every bit my African Uncle: his love for our continent ran deep, his celebration of our Black roots was vibrant; his day-to-day life embraced the culture of our ancestors. In a way, he gave me permission to celebrate the Black blood barely visible within me.

12

AS I GREW OLDER, MY SOFT GOLDEN CURLS turned into tiny ringlets that were Afro-puffy when combed through. I cannot count the number of combs Mummy and Granny bent or broke, trying to tame it. I had never been subject to the pencil test—both my parents were Coloured, so I automatically received the Coloured stamp of disapproval the day I was born—but if I had been, my ringlets would have wrapped themselves around the pencil and held on tight, like ivy twining around a tree.

By age nine, my hair had grown to an extraordinary thickness and was the defining feature of my physical appearance.

Like me, Mummy had naturally kinky hair, but she kept every strand bone-straight with the help of chemical relaxers. At night, she swirled her hair around her head then wrapped it in a *doek* or headscarf, or a pair of nylon stockings with the legs cut off and tied, which was the cheaper alternative favored by many Coloured women. This was a common method for preserving straightened hair, as the *doek* kept one's locks in place and natural frizz at bay during sleep.

The power of straight hair was so profound that Coloured women seldom wore their hair in its natural state and went to great lengths to keep it straight. Harsh chemicals and blow-drying were part of routine beauty management, and spending hours and hours on hair maintenance was standard.

For Coloured women, moisture was not a loyal friend: water and humidity revealed the truth about processed hair. Mummy kept far away from pools and swimming in the ocean for fear that her hair would "go back home." "Ooh child, my *hares* will go back home if I go in there," she would say. "I don't want to look like a *crus kop*." Similar comments, ones that disparaged Black physical traits and elevated White ones as the pinnacle of beauty, were common within the Coloured community at large: "You are so lucky to have good hair!" or "You are blessed to have fair skin."

Whether they admitted it or not, almost everyone around me desired more "European" features: straighter hair, fairer skin, lighter eyes. This was not mere vanity, nor some superficial desire: in Apartheid South Africa, such features had great power. When a dark-skinned classmate once asked me if my fair eyes had special powers, I answered, cruelly, that they let me see in the dark. At the time, I thought the girl ignorant for such a question, but in retrospect, her question demonstrated a better understanding of our Apartheid reality than my response. My light skin, light eyes and blonde hair, inherited from my maternal great-grandmother's Welsh lover and the European soldier on my father's side, gave me the power to change my life for the better. As an adult, inclination and a chemical hair straightener would have been all I needed to follow Aunty Val's example and live as a White person. But I was more inclined to Uncle Nicki's position than Aunty Val's, and though the world of Apartheid South Africa served up rude reminders of my non-White—and therefore inferior—status, I always thought of being "Coloured" with pride and never gave much thought, if any at all, to my physical appearance— until Marcel entered our life.

He called me "Rolux Magnum."

This was a nickname from a television advertisement for a lawnmower. At first, I thought it was a good commercial but soon came to hate it.

The commercial began with a European man pushing a lawnmower through the high grass of the South African *veldt*. He was followed by a crew of African men carrying his belongings. After a few seconds, they stumbled across another European man, who was meant to be Henry Stanley, the journalist who went in search of the famous explorer, Dr. Livingston. Upon their encounter, the Stanley character enthusiastically exclaimed, "Dr. Livingston, I presume!"

"Wrong presumption, this time. It's 'Rolux Magnum,'" the man with the lawnmower responded. Pointing behind him to a long, freshly mowed path, he continued, "What else can cut a path from Cape to Cairo? It turns African jungle into tabletop lawn." He said this with a smile, as the African men with him sang to the words, "*Rolux Magnum.*"

Marcel found the commercial funny in relation to my hair. "Finally, something capable of cutting that mop on your head," he would laugh. I tried my best to pretend his comments didn't bother me, but it must have been obvious how upset I was. Otherwise, he wouldn't have been so relentless with his taunting. Simply walking past him warranted a smack on my bum, followed by, "Hey! Rolux Magnum, the jungle you call hair needs a good mow." Then he would laugh so hard he'd almost fall out of his chair. Sometimes I wished he would.

With all his teasing, I began to dislike my hair and wanted it to be straight and smooth. Tania's hair fell in long, smooth curls. Thurn kept his short, although if left to grow to any length, it rippled gently. They had none of the kinkiness I inherited. I thought maybe, if my hair were straight like theirs, Marcel would leave me alone.

I spent a lot of time combing my curly hair in hopes of making it straight, but it was as tamable as an African Buffalo, and all the combing only intensified its volume. So I wore it close to my scalp and kept it wrapped in a tight bun or in plaits.

Then Mummy started chemically straightening my hair. The chemicals were harsh, and it took a long time, but I didn't mind. Mummy was not one to talk back to anyone, especially Marcel, but this was her way of helping me so that he would stop the teasing. It worked, but things got worse.

I'M NINE OR TEN YEARS OLD, AND MARCEL CALLS me out to his car. "Gillian," Marcel says. "I want to teach you how to properly clean a car."

Despite how much I had disliked cleaning Uncle Johnny's car, at this moment I would give anything to have him teaching me, I would even welcome him telling me how I should "always keep a smile on my dial," because I know cleaning Marcel's car, whatever that entails, will be much, much worse.

"Yes, Marcel." I drag my feet as I follow him outside.

The car is parked on the side of the house, where the lemon trees grow. "Get in the passenger side," Marcel says.

I do as instructed. He climbs into the driver's side. I am now sitting across from him, and I feel very uncomfortable. He has brought no cleaning supplies.

He pulls out a magazine I have never before seen in my life. He opens it and shows it to me. It contains photos of naked adults. I'm confused as to what this has to do with cleaning, but I think maybe it is like when the toilet paper is all gone at the end of the month, and we have to clean our bums with newspaper: first, you rip a page from the newspaper, then rub it between both hands to soften the sharp edges until it is ready for use. Maybe we're using the magazine paper to clean the car.

But Marcel doesn't rip any pages from the magazine. Instead, he opens to a different page and points to a naked lady with her legs spread and her hand on her private parts. Right then, I know we are not cleaning the car. He has tricked me. I turn my head away in embarrassment, and he says, "Don't look away. You must look at these pictures. Will you do this when you're grown up?" He points to the very bad picture.

I am in shock. My body feels frozen, and my mind slows, but my heart is racing. As I sit motionless, he leans into me. I can feel his hot breath on my face and his wet tongue on my dry lips. Nobody has ever taught me about such things, but I know what is happening is very wrong. I don't think to open the door and jump out. Instead, the world tilts in a way that makes me feel as if I'm going to pass out.

His tongue makes its way into my mouth, and I bite down hard. He pushes me against the car door. "What the bladdy hell is wrong with you?"

I open the door and run.

I don't know what has just happened. Have I done the right or wrong thing? I feel a heavy guilt. I worry. How can I confess this at church on Saturday? What would I say? Maybe I will explain how he is the devil. But the devil lives in Hell, not in our house, so how is Father Barnard going to believe me? I am confused because I am not even sure what I would be confessing, but mostly I am embarrassed.

I decide not to confess. I keep the bite a secret, and Marcel doesn't say anything about it either.

Though he doesn't try to kiss me again, he is never far away. There is a small hole in the bathroom door he refuses to fix, so I stuff toilet paper in there when I take a bath, but sometimes it falls out, and I know it is him on the other side. I look through it from the other side, just to see what he can see. The hole is small, but I have a good view of the entire bathroom.

My hair is straight, and the teasing has stopped, but I still have to be very careful around Marcel.

13

OUTSIDE OF THE GREENWOOD PARK HOUSE, the violence of Apartheid South Africa raged: mass uprisings, police brutality, nationwide State of Emergencies, hotel bombings, restaurant bombings, grocery store bombings, and car bombings.

South Africa was in the throes of change.

When Marcel first mentioned the idea of us relocating to America, Granny was thrilled.

"This will be a great opportunity for you children. South Africa is going to Hell in a handbasket. With all the goings-on here, you children don't stand a chance. *Ag man,* it's just too terrible for words. People are dying left, right, and center—and my God, my poor child. Nicki is going to die, and I can't have all my children's blood shed on this soil. All I can do is just pray to the Good Lord for a miracle." She made the sign of the cross. Granny had been *frot* with worry since Nicki called to tell us how his car, which had gone missing a couple of months ago, was then returned under very strange circumstances.

"So, a policeman shows up at my house and says, 'Are you Nicholas Tucker?' I say yes. He then proceeds to ask me if I own a 16-seat minibus. Of course, I say, yes, I have reported it stolen. The cop tells me they've found my missing van, and I will need to come down to the police station to retrieve it. So, I go, and sure enough, the van is there, but I notice all my AZAPO paperwork is missing. This is very concerning because it includes the Gauteng Branch's confidential information. To make this whole thing short, it's around suppertime when I get home from the police station. I park the car in the driveway and go inside. Gabi has supper ready, and I'm just about to sit down when I hear an explosion outside, and my neighbor comes running over, yelling and screaming. And I know right away it was intended for me to be inside the *kombi* when the bomb went off."

It turned out an explosive device had been inserted into the petrol tank. This convinced Granny that it was only a matter of time before Nicki was killed. Granny never spoke of Monica's death from crossing the street at seven years old, but with the death of her next youngest virtually assured by his political activity, Granny must have felt it just a matter of time before South Africa took all her children from her.

With Marcel talking of moving to America, Granny was only too happy to hand over the last of her savings to make our trip possible. She had scraped together every last Rand she had and bought our one-way airplane tickets out of Hell. To her mind, Marcel was our "savior," leading us to the promised land, where the sidewalks were paved in gold.

Uncle Nicki said we were headed into the "Belly of the Beast."

Nicki's negative opinion aside, I had heard that America was a great place. In conversations with friends, we talked about how "cool" it was that American students didn't wear school uniforms, and there were apparently lots of jobs, no matter the colour of your skin. My friend Melanie said, "There is no such thing as 'Whites only' over there."

Nicki begged to differ. "Don't be fooled. Even in America, a nigger is still a nigger." I had the utmost respect and admiration for Nicki, so when he spoke about America, I listened. After all, except for Aunty Val, he was the only one in our family who had ever been to America, and her position on the subject of Whites and Coloureds could not have been more different from Nicki's. I loved Aunty Val, deeply, but "If you can't beat 'em, join 'em" was not a position I could get behind. Especially not when it came to Mummy and Marcel.

Mummy and Marcel had left South Africa a month before so they could get things settled at our new residence in California. Granny and Uncle Johnny moved into the house in Greenwood Park to look after us and make all the necessary preparations for us to leave. Granny fretted for weeks about what we would do if our passports and visas were not approved, given that Nicki was on the government's watch list.

Secretly, I wished we'd never have to leave South Africa; Mummy could stay in California with Marcel, and we would be safe with Granny and Uncle Johnny. I had developed a greater appreciation for Uncle Johnny since living with Marcel.

I didn't want to live in America, especially not with Marcel. I didn't want to say goodbye to Granny, to Uncle Nicki and Aunty Val, to my friends, to Greenwood Park, to Durban, or to the sparkling Indian Ocean. But when we got our passports, and Granny bought each of us children a huge plastic duffle bag to pack our things for our move to America, I knew I didn't have a choice.

It was 1986 when we took our final drive in Uncle Johnny's car. I was fourteen years old, and once again, Thurn, Tania, and I were sitting in the back seat of a car. This time, we were being driven to the Durban Bus Station, where we would be dropped off and shuttled to Johannesburg. We would spend the night with Aunty Val at her flat then fly to America.

Sitting in the car with Granny, on our way to this new and foreign country, this place Uncle Nicki has so condemned, I chafed against her exuberance for America and her condemnation of South Africa. Nicki had disappeared after the incident with the minibus, and while Granny speculated that he was in Botswana again, I didn't think this was the case, because one of the last things I remembered Nicki saying was, "A revolution must be waged inside a country."

"WELL, PERSONALLY, *I* THINK WHAT NICKI'S DOING is commendable. We need more people like him. What's been done in the name of Apartheid is one of humanity's worst ills. The racist regime must be stopped."

Granny turns and looks at me in surprise. "*Ag*, Gillian, you mustn't talk such nonsense," she says. "You sound like Nicki, and look at the trouble he is in. You children must get out of here now. You can't even think about these things. Don't think about it, please, my child. It's a death wish."

She is silent, lost deep in thought for a moment. Then she adds, "*Ay*, my poor, poor son. What a crying shame. *Eish!*"

As I board the plane for golden shores, I can't think of where I'm going, only of what I'm leaving.

I'm leaving Granny and all her worries.

I'm leaving Nicki, his comrades, and a brewing revolution.

I'm leaving Aunty Val and the enemies she rubs shoulders with.

I'm leaving my friends.

I'm leaving my mango tree.

I'm leaving Father's body buried somewhere in the African dirt.

Nisale Kahle Afrika.

AMERICA

"I am going to be me as I am, and you can beat me or jail me or even kill me, but I'm not going to be what you want me to be." —Steve Biko

Ventura, California

14

I LIVED AMONG THIEVES.

You know of Marcel who lurked and hovered over every crack in the door and every sliver of light.

Moving to America changed none of that.

You know of Apartheid, the beast that fed its White heart with the blood of Africans, Coloureds, and Indians.

Moving to America just swapped one beast for another.

Please don't misunderstand. I am not equating Cold War America with Apartheid South Africa. The great white shark cruising South African coasts and the bison roaming American plains are both beasts, but dangerous in very different ways. Where one feeds on flesh and blood and will travel eighty kilometers in search of a kill, the other keeps to itself and will attack only when it feels threatened.

An attack is still an attack.

We were enrolled at Buena High School in the city of Ventura, on the coast north of Los Angeles. This was quite a shock to my world. To start, the majority of the student body was White. On top of which, many of them didn't understand me when I spoke, even though I spoke English, and those who did understand asked me the most ignorant questions I had ever heard.

"What language are you speaking?"

"But, like, I thought only *Black people* live in Africa?"

"Yeah, did you like buy your clothes at the *airport*?" This was one of the more ignorant questions I was asked based on the presumption people in Africa did not wear clothing. I blame National Geographic magazine for that one.

"Do they say bitch in Africa? Can you say bitch? Say bitch." *Sure. I can even do you one better and add a 'fuck you' in front of that 'bitch.' Bitch.*

"Where did you learn English?" *Gee, let's see. Where did you learn English? Oh, family and school? So odd but the same here; we must have so much in common.*

"Where *is* South Africa?" Now I never expected Americans to have knowledge about my country's history, but this question left me speechless.

I struggled to find a group where I could express myself freely. Initially, I gravitated toward African Americans. They looked familiar to me, like all the people I grew up with. I'll fit in with them and figure things out, I thought. It didn't take long for me to learn I was not their "girlfriend."

"Hey, girlfriend!"

"Yes?"

"I ain't talkin' to you."

"Oh, I'm sorry."

"Yeah, you *better* be."

I was surprised to learn they did not consider me one of them. In South Africa, as my father's experience showed, Black and White was more than skin colour, it was blood. In America, with my blonde hair, fair skin, and a British-sounding accent, Blacks could only see me as White.

The tragic irony is that the South African system for classifying race was a more honest system than the one my siblings and I had to navigate in America. You see, in America, no one recognized the Zulu blood which ran through my veins because they couldn't see it in my skin. I quickly learned that my blackness, though no longer a liability, was not even acknowledged in America. I was Coloured, but America refused to see it.

In America, Coloured is a term reminiscent of the Jim Crow Era, and the Civil Rights Movement disposed of that term when it tore down the signs. When my family immigrated to America in 1986, you were either Black or White, and because I looked White, I was identified White, despite the fact that I was no more White than the White girls at my school were Black, and I was not about to play White just to fit in in America.

Since the Blacks didn't want anything to do with me, and since I didn't want anything to do with the Whites, I gravitated toward the Mexicans. The Mexicans had brown skin just like many Coloured people, and from what I knew, many of them were illegal, just like me.

We had arrived in America as tourists, moving into a two-bedroom apartment. Within six months, our visas expired, making us "illegal aliens." I certainly felt like an alien among the valley girls and surfers of this strange land. Mummy forbade us from talking to anyone about being illegal, so I tacked that onto my growing list of secrets.

"No one can ever know of our immigration status," Mummy said, "or we'll be deported, and Granny's hard-earned savings will have been wasted."

I'M WITH TIFFANY, A GIRL FROM THE APARTMENT complex I've befriended. We're riding our bikes within a nearby reservoir enclosed by a chain-link fence when we're confronted by four Mexican girls.

"What you looking at, *gringos*?" one of them asks.

I look around to see who the Mexican girls are talking to and realize that Tiffany and I are the only ones in the enclosed reservoir.

"We're not looking at anyone," I say.

"You looking at me right now."

"Because you asked me a question."

"You being smart with me, *gringo*?"

Something in their eyes reminds me of Marcel. There is a well of rage so deep, I know any answer I give will be wrong. I drop my bike and run for the open gate. Tiffany pedals ahead of me. The four girls follow in pursuit. We make it through the gate, and I get as far as the middle of the street outside the reservoir before the girls pounce on me, kicking and pulling my hair in different directions.

Tiffany is still pedaling toward the apartment complex, and I yell after her, "Go get my mother! Call the police!"

We escaped South Africa only for me to get killed in the middle of a street, I think. *What a waste of a plane ticket.*

Then suddenly, like Granny with her bush knife screaming in Zulu and slashing at the brush, Mummy is there, pulling the girls off me and screaming, "Leave my daughter alone!" Soon the police arrive, but by then, my attackers have fled, and I sit trembling on the sidewalk. I give them a full report.

One of them turns to Mummy and asks, "Do you give permission for your daughter to ride in the back of our vehicle to see if we can identify the suspects?"

When she says yes, I can hardly believe it. What is she thinking? We are supposed to avoid the police. What if they ask for my immigration documents? The last thing I want to do is get into their car, but Mummy has already told the policeman yes, and it will be suspicious if I say no. I have to act calm.

Sitting in the back seat of the patrol car, I am more nervous than I was being attacked. I am certain that any moment one of them is going to ask for my documents. They probably just forgot to ask me earlier, with all the commotion of Mummy crying.

I scan the surroundings as the police officers have told me to do, keeping an eye out so I can identify the suspects. As we drive the orderly, palm-lined streets of Ventura, I am once again struck by the foreignness of this alien country.

The neighborhood is humdrum, devoid of the lively clamor of Durban street vendors and the abundant flora of my home. Houses line the street like chunky fence posts. Every yard, park, or patch of grass is perfectly manicured. If it is attractive, it is attractive in the way the numbers on a digital clock are attractive. It is uniform and clean.

There is nothing but the sun to remind me of Africa.

Then I see them. All four of the girls casually walking the grey paved sidewalk as though they had not just beaten a stranger in the street.

I blurt out, "There they are!" and the car pulls up next to them. It is the tallest of the girls who turns and sees the police car first. For some reason, they don't run. Perhaps they don't realize they left a witness? I certainly never expected we would actually find them, and relief slips over me like a warm bath.

The car stops. The girls are arrested, and my British-sounding, White-looking, terrified, illegal self is let out of the car and free to walk back.

DESPITE THE STRANGE NEW WORLD OUTSIDE, inside our rented apartment in Ventura, things weren't much different from how they'd been in South Africa. Marcel still gripped the house, and everyone in it, in a choke-hold, and Mummy still marinated her sorrows in brandy.

The apartment was a two-story, two-bedroom set-up. Both bedrooms were upstairs, and so was the only bathroom. Mummy and Marcel slept in one bedroom, and Tania and I shared the other, just as we always had. Downstairs was a small living room, kitchen, and eating area. Thurn slept under the staircase, behind the television. It was crowded, but we had lived in smaller places.

Marcel worked for a machine shop sharpening commercial blades. I cannot tell you what his shop looked like or where in Ventura it was located, because I did not care one bit what he did outside of the roof we lived under.

Mummy worked at a small women's boutique, but the job was short-lived as the owner went out of business, so Mummy stuck to what she knew best: cooking and cleaning.

Thurn and I worked illegally at a local fast-food burger place earning minimum wage. Tania was thirteen and too young to work.

Reagan was president and had signed The Immigration Reform and Control Act into law, which criminalized the hiring of undocumented immigrants and established penalties for those doing so. We had been warned away from the weekend swap meet, held in the open lot across from our apartment complex. "I heard there was another raid last weekend," Mummy said. "The police came in and took a bunch of illegal Mexicans away in vans."

Raids were happening all around us. It was terrifying.

In Ventura, there was no mango tree to escape to. No ocean to look at from the front yard. I retreated further into my imagination. I would have picture-perfect thoughts about never again seeing Marcel. I imagined him leaving for work, and while he was away, we would pack our bags. Giddy with excitement, Mummy, Tania, and I would laugh about the expression on his face when he came back to see we had left. I imagined I would take Mummy's red lipstick and write in bold letters on the glass mirror covering the small dining room wall: *"We Are Gone and Never Coming Back. Oh, and Fuck You!"* We were not permitted to use bad language, so this message never failed to put a private smile on my face.

I also entertained grand thoughts about getting our paperwork processed and becoming legal residents so I could earn a living wage and be anywhere but living with Marcel.

Another fantasy of mine was coming back from school and learning he had been run over by a car earlier in the day. The details were slow and lovely as each sweet daydream danced into the next.

In this way, I moved through life, pretending all was well. Imagination was my mental Dettol.

Pretending was a choice, and I had become good at it over the years. After all, if I were to face my unhappiness, how could it possibly have helped? Instead, I kept the inside of my head as orderly as Granny kept her house, unhappiness tucked neatly away in sealed boxes behind locked doors.

When I did allow my mind to run free—confident I could shut the door on wild thoughts whenever I chose—I would almost immediately see the futility of indulging this way of thinking. Sure, I could open my mouth, but I was illegal, and if I did, I would be arrested. I could run away, but where would I go? The only other place I knew was South Africa, and I had neither the money nor means to get there. Being in America was like being stuck inside Uncle Johnny's car on the way to iFafa. I could have jumped out if I chose, but then what?

IT'S FRIDAY NIGHT. I'VE JUST GOTTEN OFF WORK, and I'm headed for the beach in my Ford Pinto, a shabby, brown, hatchback. "Let's Go" by *The Cars* blasts from the stereo, and I belt out the lyrics. When I get to the beach, it's too dark to see anything, but this does not bother me. I only come here Friday nights to be somewhere else until I have to make the inevitable U-turn and drive back to the house on Portola Road.

15

THURN AND TANIA SEEMED TO EFFORTLESSLY blend in with their White classmates. Thurn had joined the (all White) tennis team at school, and Tania was a scorekeeper at basketball and other such games.

Not me. I still carried a heavy Apartheid chip that contributed to a growing divide between my siblings and me. "Why can't you just try?" Tania would ask. And I tried. I really did. But rubbing shoulders with the White enemy felt wrong. I knew it would be disappointing to Nicki and, ultimately, myself.

In South Africa, I was Coloured. In America, I was an *illegal alien* which was even worse. I found the term exceptionally demoralizing, and I did not embrace it as I did the word Coloured. I loved the idea of being considered a colour or string of colours, each with its unique beauty. No human should be called either illegal or alien. The only thing I saw as illegal was what Marcel was doing to me. But here we were.

I blamed Marcel for bringing us to this foreign place. It seemed to me he knew exactly what he was doing. He had isolated us even further, to do with as he wished. If he was going to continue abusing me, at least it could be in a country where I belonged. Where I was comfortable. Where if people did not like you, they simply did not smile at you. I missed my friends, my family, my mango tree. I missed hearing people talk openly about topics of race and religion. In America, such topics are considered taboo.

A teacher once asked me how different South Africa was to America in terms of race and I told her that in South Africa when someone does not like the colour of your skin, they will tell you so, but in America, people will smile to your face and say something different when your back is turned. White people often think others don't notice what they do, but we do. We remember more than they might like us to.

STANDING AT MY LOCKER, I WATCH TWO GIRLS smile and greet a Black student on her way to the bathroom. I wait to see what they will do once the Black girl's passed, and I am not surprised to see their smiles drop.

One of them says to the other, "Yeah, like, I would never go to Ventura High School. There are so many more Blacks there."

"Right! And like so many Mexicans, too."

In my silent judgment, I question my own smiling mask and wonder if I am any different than these girls.

We are swimming for PE, and I hate it. Last week I lied and said that I could not swim because I was on my period. I can't use the same excuse this week.

For years now, I have chemically straightened my hair and kept it straight by blow-drying it weekly behind closed doors. It takes me at least an hour and a half to straighten my hair with a blow-dryer. Getting it wet will undo all the work I put into it, so I have devised a plan to keep it dry when I swim. I have bought a swim cap, and I neatly tuck my hair under the cap. As I walk out onto the hot concrete pool top of Buena High School, Ventura, California, my classmates turn in my direction and laugh.

"I didn't know anyone wore swim caps except for old people," one of the girls says. The laughter continues. It's humiliating, but I'll take it over subjecting my hair to the pool and having everyone see it change into a kinky mop before their eyes. And I don't have an hour and a half between classes to blow-dry it straight. So, the next day I return with my cap and swallow the pill of laughter.

My hair stays straight.

FROM THE TIME HE MOVED IN WITH US, MARCEL claimed to be in constant back pain. If he did not receive a massage two to three times a week—from me, in his underwear—all hell broke loose. I lived with this revolting man from the time I was eight years old: this man who crept into a child's room at night and touched her. I was fourteen when I decided I had reached my limit. Though I was still afraid of him, I was done. I would not touch his back again or let him touch me.

I knew refusing Marcel would mean saying no. Saying no to an adult was disrespectful, and children were never permitted to speak disrespectfully to their elders, but I no longer cared.

I AM IN MARCEL AND MUMMY'S BEDROOM, WHERE he has summoned me. He lies on the bed wearing just his underwear. His legs are crossed at the ankles.

"Rub my back," he says. That is all.

Have you ever wondered what causes the explosive bang from a popped balloon? It is a sound wave created by the release of high-pressure air from inside the balloon displacing the lower-pressure air around it as it expands.

By rough estimate, this is the 612th "Rub my back," a nearly-nude Marcel has hurled at me. Coupled with countless nights of cocooning myself in blankets to defend against his brutish, tearing hands and wet breath, I have reached my breaking point. All the pressure built up from years of abuse is released, and without even thinking, I scream for Mummy: "Mummy, come here!"

I hear Mummy's feet pattering up the stairs. "What is it?" she calls. Her voice sounds panicked. I hadn't planned to do this, and I don't know what to expect. What if I'm punished?

Mummy bursts through the door, and I hear myself scream, "I can't take this anymore!" What happens next surprises me even more.

I begin to cry.

I didn't cry when Mummy snuck away through the brush after abandoning us at Granny's. That was Tania. I didn't cry on the way to iFafa when I found out Father was dead, though I had wanted to. I didn't cry at Mr. and Mrs. Fayes' when weekend after weekend passed without a visit from Mummy, even though Granny wasn't there to tell me that a lady doesn't cry.

Yet with Mummy standing in front of me, tears fill my eyes. I blink. A tear breaks free. The floodgates open, and

I choke out words between sobs. "Do you know what he's been doing to me? He makes me rub his back dressed like THAT!" I point to Marcel, still lying on the bed in his underwear. I realize I'm wailing now, so I pause to compose myself, draw in a deep breath, and continue. "And he comes into our room at night. He waits until I fall asleep and comes into the room and touches me under the covers." My voice is raw—anger cracks through my tears. I turn and point a trembling finger at Marcel. "And DON'T LIE!"

Marcel says nothing.

"It's not right," I say, each word an indictment. I turn to Mummy for reassurance. She is staring at me. I watch her eyes widen, like someone pushing open a window. Fear creeps in to join the rage. "It's not right," I repeat, still looking up at her. "Right?"

Her eyes glimmer beneath eyebrows she still plucks to wispy lines she fills in softly with pencil. She says nothing. I will have to finish this myself.

I turn back to Marcel, my voice desperate. "I just . . . I just want you to stop."

Mummy is sobbing next to me, which, for some reason, gives me the confidence to continue. Perhaps because her tears are such a familiar part of the Marcel equation, except this time, I will not be comforting her.

Marcel lies stiffly on the bed, legs still crossed. He stares out the window.

"Why have you been doing this to me?"

His eyes remain fixed on the clear blue sky in front of him, and without moving or turning his head, he says in a tone as brittle as ice, "Because you're not my biological daughter."

He turns to look at me, and before I can say another word, he takes a deep breath, and his fat nostrils flare. He looks as if he could lunge at me any moment, but I hold my position beside the bed. Slowly he turns to Mummy, who is still crying. She attempts to say something, but he cuts her off. It seems as though he has heard enough from both of us.

"Shut up and listen here, both of you," he says. "If you ever mention this to anybody, I promise I will make all of you regret you ever lived. I will get all of you deported. You will lose everything. I will lie about this until the day I die. Now get out of my sight."

Two days later, a sexual abuse hotline number is hung on the fridge. Mummy must have put it there. The following day it is removed.

He never comes into my bedroom again.

Reno, Nevada

16

I T IS SAID THAT THE SUN, THE MOON, AND THE truth can't be long hidden. Keeping up a smiling facade had become difficult. The tidy compartments inside my head had begun to feel messy, and the tightly closed doors had begun to come ajar.

My naked confession must have let out the churning grease because afterward, my head felt tidy again. It felt good to no longer have to tightly wrap my body in blankets each night.

We moved to Reno the year I turned nineteen. I had graduated high school, and Marcel had big plans of opening his own machine shop sharpening commercial blades. He said this line of business was growing and there was a big market for it in Reno. I barely listened when he spoke, and no longer pretended I cared. As long as he had a job that took him away from the house each day, I was satisfied. The house he and Mummy purchased was a rather nondescript affair. It was a 1950s single story with three bedrooms, a narrow kitchen, and a sunroom attached to the living room in the back of the house. It looked like most other houses in the neighborhood, but where others might have been homes, ours was a house. The only warmth came from the Reno heat or the living room fireplace we put to use in the winter months.

Marcel eventually opened his own shop, and Tania began working for him. Now that she had her driver's license, she would pick up orders, deliver sharpened saws to his customers, and engage in administrative tasks. She was still the dutiful daughter but no longer the little sister who followed me around.

A year after moving to Reno, we won the biggest prize an illegal alien can win: the Green Card Lottery. Every year the US Department of State randomly selects immigration entries and awards visas to individuals from countries with low rates of immigration to the United States. In 1990, South Africa was on the list of eligible countries, and our paperwork had risen to the top like cream.

With this new freedom to live honestly and openly, I thirsted for even more. I worked as many jobs as possible to gain the independence I craved. With my new immigration status, I was no longer a criminal in the United States of America, and I didn't have to settle for the lowest-paying jobs. Being legal felt like having a buffet of employment to choose from, and I took my first bites at two quintessentially enormous American companies: Albertsons and UPS.

I spent mornings unloading trailers for UPS and afternoons and evenings as a cashier at Albertsons. Each day began at four a.m., when I would report to a giant warehouse with twenty- and forty-foot containers backed up to openings in the wall. For four hours, I unloaded my assigned trailer, placing packages on moving belts. I was the only female unloader on the floor, and my first week on the job, the other unloaders at the UPS Reno warehouse placed bets on how long I would last.

"No way she'll last even a week."

"Two days. I'd say she's about a hundred and twenty pounds, and those fifty-pound packages are going to kill her."

Little did they know the price I had paid for the job. They weren't aware of the hunger and ambition roiling inside me. For years I'd worked illegally for minimum wage. No way would I lose a job paying $10 an hour.

I saved my money. I had plans to move out of the house as soon as possible and hopefully attend college. Each morning I took in the Nevada air like a baby taking her first breaths. No longer would I be dependent on my mother or Marcel. The fortune promised me nearly two decades ago by the mystical shroud I had worn that hot June afternoon in Durban, South Africa seemed, for the first time in many years, to be mine.

Marcel had always hated me. The way he looked at me was not the way he looked at Tania or even Thurn. When he looked at me, he never bothered to hide the ugliness in his eyes; he *wanted* me to see it. For a long time, I thought it was just me he hated and often wondered why. Was it because I bit his tongue? Was it the needles I stuck in the carpet around my side of the bed? Which is another story I would like to tell you.

January 1, 1982. We'd been living in the house on 19 Sentinel Avenue, Greenwood Park for almost two years. Mummy's birthday was the 12th of January, and Tania and I had been saving our pennies for a birthday present. Mummy would give us five cents here and there to buy ourselves a piece of candy at the local tearoom, but instead, we saved.

The day before Mummy's birthday, we had one Rand and fifty cents to spend on a gift. Tania and I walked down Effingham Road to the local chemist as pleased with ourselves as if we held a Kruger Rand in each pocket. When we reached the chemist, we browsed the shelves looking for a special gift for Mummy.

"How about this glass rose?" Tania asked.

"How much is it?"

Turning the rose over Tania said, "Two Rand and twenty-five-cents."

"Too expensive."

Time began to dissolve with the rain outside until we found a momentous gift we could afford; a porcelain turtle with a cushioned shell to stick pins in. Though Granny enjoyed sewing, Mummy was not one to sew, but how could she not like this turtle with its accompanying packet of pins? And, it was one Rand! We would even have money left over for a card.

Mummy loved her gift, though she had little use for it. She kept the turtle on her nightstand while I made use of the pins.

TANIA IS ASLEEP. I SNEAK OUT THE PACKET OF PINS I have hidden under my pillow. In the dark and on my knees, I carefully place each pin into the red carpet with the head of the pin facing down and the needle end sticking straight up. Pins surround my side of the bed like warriors with spears protecting Shaka's Zulu Kingdom.

Now I will know for sure if my nightmares are real or not.

I wake to Marcel, hollering "Bladdy hell!" in my room. It is too dark to see him, but I know what has happened. I tense under the blankets I wrap tightly around myself each night, but he doesn't come any closer. I hear a click, and he is gone.

Of course, I cannot keep the pins there, or Tania could get injured. Or she might ask me why they're there. I remove them before she wakes the next morning.

THE NOCTURNAL VISITS DIDN'T STOP, WHICH WAS fine; I could manage. He only targeted me. If he had targeted Tania, I would have felt very different, but in all the years Tania and I shared a bedroom, I never woke up to see him on her side of the bed, only mine. In fact, I never saw him do anything to Tania—no sideways glances or secret smiles.

Yes, it was only me he hated.

Outside of closed doors, Marcel presented well in front of others. Keeping a polished image was of paramount importance to him, and many were deceived by his charm. Certainly, Mummy had been. And Granny.

Tania, Thurn, and I never spoke to each other of the abuse we lived with for years, and I had never spoken to Tania of the sexual abuse Marcel inflicted on me. Though Thurn, Tania, and I were siblings, we'd never shared such a bond. Each of us survived independently and did not lean on one another for comfort, shelter, or confidence. We were not each other's keepers; instead, we stood, soundlessly, at our own gates, keeping watch lest one or the other draw too close. For reasons I don't entirely understand, Tania, Thurn, and I, very early on, found protection in disconnecting from each other.

Ironically, the closer I got to realizing my dream of living away from Marcel, the more I came to notice Tania and Thurn. Thurn, who had always been quieter than Tania and me, now barely spoke at all. Where he had been distant, he was now absent: present, but unaccounted for. Tania had gone to the other extreme, keeping as polished an image of light and smiles as Marcel. She worked at his machine shop, doing all his pick-ups, deliveries, and billing. She seemed happy enough, but the more I considered how manipulative and cunning Marcel was, the more I began to worry that he may have shifted his attacks to an easier target.

I didn't like that Tania was working for him now, and I began to wonder.

"TANIA, I NEED TO TALK TO YOU AWAY FROM THE HOUSE."

"About what?"

"Can we go on a walk, and I'll tell you?"

"Okay."

It is winter. We walk through the hills around our Reno neighborhood. The trees stand calm and peaceful as sunlight arrows through their naked branches. Dry leaves crackle underfoot.

I begin. "I need to talk to you about something that's been on my mind."

"What is it?"

"Did . . . did he ever touch you?"

"Who?"

"Marcel."

"What do you mean?"

"I mean, when we lived in South Africa and Ventura, Marcel used to come into our room at night and touch me under the covers. Did he do the same to you?"

Tania doesn't answer. She looks at the ground. I stare at the trees.

We walk on for a while in silence. She seems preoccupied with the sidewalk in front of her.

I ask her again.

"Did he ever touch you? Please tell me. I swear I will never tell another soul. I *just need to know.*"

Tania sighs and looks into the horizon. "Gillian, why can't you ever just let the past be the past? Why must you always try to fix things?"

I'm not trying to fix anything. I just want her to give me an answer. I just want to hear that he hasn't touched her, that she's never seen or heard anything, that she is the soundest sleeper in history. Nothing would make me happier than for Tania to look me in the eye and tell me that I am walking through this fire without her.

I beg. "Please talk to me, Tania. Tell me."

"I don't want to talk about it." The ground seems to have hypnotized her as we walk.

"Please, Tania. I've never asked you for anything. And right now, I am begging you. Talk to me, please. I'm your sister."

Tears begin to roll down her cheeks.

She turns to me, and she says, "If you ever tell anyone, I will never talk to you again. I swear, Gillian. I will never forgive you."

"I understand. I promise."

She stops walking. She does not look at me or even in my direction.

"Yes, he touched me," she tells the cold pavement in front of her. "Whenever he took just me on those fun runs, or when I'm at his workshop . . ."

A hum enters my head, and I can no longer hear her. Tania continues to speak, and I watch her lips move, but I hear nothing. My eardrums swell to bursting, and my hands begin to shake. My vision blurs. I have my answer, but it's not what I wanted. Now what?

"Gillian!"

"Yes, I'm listening."

"Now promise me you'll never say anything to any-one." With tears smeared over her face, my sister looks like she has been dragged behind a car.

"I promise," I lie.

Tania resumes walking, and I follow her numbly through suburbia where one tract house blends into another under a blank and dreary sky.

17

ONCE AGAIN, FORTUNE HAS ELUDED ME.

In all my ignorance, I had thought it was Marcel's hatred of me that made me a target. All those years, he had picked on *my* hair, not Tania's. He hated *me*. I should have known better—God, how I should have known.

I had spent so much time protecting Mummy when I should have been protecting Tania.

Tania was an easy target. She was very much a people-pleaser and never raised her voice at Marcel, or anyone else for that matter. We were quite different in this way. Why had I not seen any of this? How could I have been such a fool?

Now, on top of hating him, I hate Mummy.

And I hate myself.

I can't leave Marcel without Tania, and Tania won't go. I'm still trapped.

I try to put this newfound information away in my head, to store it neatly out of sight, as I've done with such things for years. I work more. I start running. I hike hills. I enroll in a community college. Still, this new secret won't be buried by distractions. It grows inside me, a malignant tumor fueled by horror, anger, guilt, pain, and rage. I wonder if it can be removed without killing its host.

Once we had become permanent residents of the United States of America, Mummy began working and saving money. She had planned a *lekker* celebration. Everyone we knew who could possibly come had been invited—family, new friends, old friends, neighbors, and acquaintances—everyone. Aunty Val, who was now living in California, would be driving up for the festivities with her American husband, Dennis. We'd even paid to fly Granny in from "Hell-in-a-handbasket" South Africa.

For Marcel, the most special guest of all would also be coming from South Africa: his father, Lenny, a one-eyed opera singer with a similar proclivity for young women.

On the day of the party, our three-bedroom Reno house was full of guests. The whole place buzzed with excitement, but I didn't share in it. I helped Mummy set out plates of food and smiled politely at family and friends, but inwardly, I celebrated nothing.

When I was young, there was a traveling circus in South Africa, the Boswell Wilkie Circus, which was very popular for many years. It was one of the first shows to allow racially mixed audiences and the first to defy

Apartheid's ban on Sunday entertainment. Tania, Thurn, and I went once. What I remembered most from that day were the animals: the dogs, elephants, and donkeys they had on display. Of course, there was also the ringmaster who introduced the famous Tickey the Clown with his painted face and floppy bush hat.

More than a decade and ten thousand miles later, this party felt like nothing so much as a circus with Marcel as ringmaster. He's a con man, a huckster, a carnival barker, who has invited everyone to applaud his performance. Everything was orchestrated. Everything a lie. The laughter was a lie. Every word out of Marcel's tight mouth was a lie. Like the ringmaster vaunting himself over a cage full of tigers which could eat him alive, Marcel has stood on the shoulders of children, using fear and abuse to control them and choosing a woman who wouldn't interfere. I had a choice: I could play the role of passive spectator as I'd done as a child; I could join Mummy, Tania, and Thurn and play the clown, a role I'd perfected in the eleven years of living with Marcel; or I could choose to be one of the circus animals—beaten, but which, having taken enough abuse, turns on its trainer.

Marcel was in the family room, talking with his father. Lenny had come to witness how successful Marcel had become. Marcel had bragged to his father on long-distance phone conversations about his business and his machine shop and the great money he was making. He swaggered and smirked through the party. He talked about how the house we lived in, with its white picket fence and roses growing in the side yard, belonged to him. And of course, he never missed an opportunity to boast about the family he "rescued" and how well we were doing now that he had taught us to be polite, respectful, and hardworking. To all appearances, he was a bright, shiny version of the immigrant success story.

Food in South Africa—or in any African nation—is a currency most Americans simply can't appreciate. Its scarcity and expense are staggering in Africa. To come from South Africa, where hunger made itself known even in homes led by working adults, and see American grocery stores with their bins of countless varieties of apples—all bright and fresh and shiny, year-round—it was no less surprising than if we had found that the streets of America were actually paved with gold. A full table in South Africa was considered an almost rude extravagance; even the poorest household with the most meager of rations knew someone who had less and would tut-tut if a feast was not shared. A party laid out with a month's worth of food would have been viewed as criminally wasteful, but in America, such extravagance was expected. There was food—lots of it.

Mummy had prepared spicy chicken curry, crab curry, lamb biryani, samosas, mango pickle, chutney, sausage rolls, milk tart, bread pudding, and freshly baked bread. It was cold out, and a fire burned in the living room. The combined smells of smoke, spicy foods, and sweet dessert reminded me of Africa. With the food and the smells and my beloved family visiting from far corners of the globe, all should have been well, or as the Americans would say, hunky-dory.

But a shadow followed me from room to room, from task to task. I found myself surprised no one else felt it. People were laughing in the kitchen, and friends and family spilled through the wide-open door to the garage, filling both rooms. A crisp chill sharpened the evening air, but even with a house full of people, and a fire blazing, I was cold. The open door let in a draft that seemed to find only me. I kept on my heavy brown leather jacket.

Across the house full of people, Marcel looked at me with his familiar crooked smile. It was a cunning smile, the smile of a jackal or a dog before it bites, a smile that matched his eyes. Normally, his smile and those eyes would have filled me with fear and made me look away, but I was no longer afraid. I was angry. The secrets I'd held inside me felt like a fire instead of a cancer; instead of killing me slowly, they fueled me. My body trembled from the flame. I wanted to grab him by his crooked smile and slam his face into the kitchen cupboard he was leaning against. I wanted to spit all the bitter ashes of my childhood—*our* childhood—into those eyes. As if he could sense the change in me, Marcel's smirk flattened into a thin, tight line. He tilted his head, like a dog perplexed by something it has never seen before. Then he turned away, and I realized I had this all wrong. He wasn't the ringmaster. He didn't run this circus. He was one of the animals: a dog which performed tricks on stage but bit anyone who came near him. Dogs don't have the power to run the show, but I did. I could end the show, put the dog down, and burn this circus to the ground.

"EXCUSE ME," I SAY. "CAN I GET EVERYONE'S ATTEN-tion?" My voice is low and calm, and the party continues on.

I shout: "Can I get everyone's attention?"

Aunty Val hears me, takes a teaspoon, and begins to clink it against her wine glass. "Gillian has an announce-ment," she says. "Let's all go in the living room." Like happy sheep, their faces flushed with food and alcohol-smoothed smiles, they file into the living room. There are so many people that few can sit down; Marcel is one of the few who do. I stand in the center of the room filled with the people I love the most. Everyone falls quiet to listen to me. There is a hiss and a pop from the wood blazing in the fireplace behind me.

"Thank you for coming. I'm glad you're all here because I have something very important to say." I take a deep breath and gesture to the room, the house, the crowd. "This is all a charade. None of this is real. The man you all know as Marcel Le Grange is really not the person who you think he is."

Faces that had looked up at me in bright expecta-tion of an announcement ("Gillian's going to honor the visiting guests from South Africa or perhaps there is a surprise guest?") stare at me, confused. Smiles slowly dissolve as I continue.

"He is a child molester. He has abused Tania and me for years. He has abused my whole family." With every word, my voice grows louder. I point directly at Marcel, sitting feet away from me, and scream, "He . . . is . . . a . . . monster!"

Marcel leaps from his seated position and lunges at me with a powerful punch. Aunty Val, standing behind me, sees him coming and pulls me back. The wind from his fist brushes past my face, just missing me.

What follows is like a boxing match, with the referees in each camp trying to control each of the fighters. Confusion has turned to outrage. Arms are wrapped around me, and I am still screaming:

"HE'S A MONSTER! LET ME GO!"

Molten anger rips through my body, and any fear I have ever felt of him falls off me like a discarded cloak. I clench my fists. I want nothing more than to feel them smash against his face, but arms are still wrapped around me. Others are holding Marcel back as he struggles to break free and get to me.

Nobody contests my words, nor voices any defense of Marcel.

I'm pulled out of the room.

I am carried out into the garage.

I fight against the arms of family and friends, trying to calm me. I want to get back inside. I'm not done with him.

I can hear Granny's voice, screaming at Marcel's father, "I knew there was something wrong with your bastard son! Both of you are bladdy rubbishers! You always liked the young girls! Pack your bags and get the fucking hell out of here! Don't just look at me, you damn glass-eyed creep. Get moving, you bastards!"

Our house is quiet the next day. Granny, who has come all the way from South Africa to celebrate, has kicked Marcel out of his own house. Without protest, he has moved into a motel with his father.

I sit on my twin bed. Mummy sits at the edge of Tania's bed. I have asked to speak with her. It is late morning, but she looks as if she has just gotten out of bed. Her disheveled hair is pulled back. She wears no makeup and looks aged. I suspect she has not slept. I haven't, but I have found my voice.

"I won't live like this anymore," I tell her. "Not a minute more. As long as he's in your life, I will not be a part of it. You have a choice, and here it is: you can remain married to him, and I walk out forever, or you can divorce him and choose your children."

Mummy's face, which has only ever shown acceptance or passive denial, contorts into a grimace. Her hands and jaw clench. Her body trembles, and just when it seems she might crumple to the floor, her mouth opens, and she bellows in a voice I've never heard her use, "Get out and leave me alone! GET OUUUUUT!"

Every ounce of anger, resentment, or fear she has ever felt toward Marcel is unleashed and directed at me. I'm in shock. It seems Mummy, too, has found her voice, and it is not human.

I stand from the edge of my bed, walk out of the room I have shared with Tania and out the front door, putting the house and all its misery behind me.

The tent has indeed burned down.

18

MUMMY WOULD EVENTUALLY DIVORCE MAR-cel, but it would take her a year to do so.

Tania and I moved into a one-bedroom apartment where I could finally breathe my own air. Never again would I take another breath under the same roof as Marcel. I had finally found freedom. This reality was exulting, yet the image of Mummy screaming at me to "get out" and choosing Marcel over her children was a searing reminder that Tania and I were being abandoned again.

I felt simultaneously unfettered and caged. I continued steady work at UPS and Albertsons. Tania no longer worked for Marcel, so I helped her secure employment at Albertsons as a checker. Though Tania and I lived together and did some things together, the divide between us continued to grow. Ever since the Marcel announcement, she cast an unspoken resentment in my direction. I had betrayed her. I shared the secret I promised never to tell. That didn't stop me from protecting her.

Tania had always been the polite one who made friends easily and eagerly smiled around others. She had a gentle way about her and an innocent belief that with enough faith, tomorrow would be better. She believed strongly in God and would rather pray than confront anyone. When a relationship she was in turned abusive, I called her boyfriend and threatened that if he came around our place again, he would regret ever meeting me. I'm not sure what I meant by this, but Tania's face gleamed when I hung up the phone. We never saw him again.

Not that Tania wasn't capable of anger and hostility. When it was just the two of us, her smiles would vanish, and my sister, who I could never remember yelling at anyone in her life, would turn on me.

"Look what you did!"

"What?"

"After your shower, you left water on the bathroom floor!"

"And?"

"And it is a mess."

"It's a couple of drops of water."

"*It is a mess!*"

At other times Tania would lord her increased sociability over me.

"I've got more friends than you," she said one day. She looked smug.

"Yes, but always remember to count your friends by the flowers that grow, not the leaves that fall."

Tania smirked and turned away.

Oh God, I was becoming Uncle Johnny.

I was still taking courses at Truckee Meadows Community College, but I wasn't satisfied. I wanted to attend a university. Driving on Virginia Street past the University of Nevada in Reno one day, I stopped and watched students walking across campus, carrying books, backpacks slung over their shoulders, chatting with each other, smiling, purposeful. I wanted to be one of those students. I wanted to make something of my life, something different from what I knew. For the first time, I could actually see myself there on UNR's campus with those students. I had no idea how to apply, or even what applying to a university entailed, but if I could get myself enrolled at a community college, I could do the same at a university.

As a child, I owned a book called *The Secret Garden*. When I read it, I marveled at the possibilities of language. In school, I would copy poems from books, and when nobody was watching, I would recite the words until I had them memorized. There was something about the written word that mesmerized me. It was mine to love, and as long as Marcel did not know of this love, he couldn't take it away from me.

Still, I heard his voice.

"You will never amount to anything."

"You're so stupid."

"You're only as good as your looks."

I sat quietly through my classes at the community college, afraid to speak. Everyone seemed so much smarter than me. I was in awe of my classmates who raised their hands and spoke with a confidence I didn't have. Most days, I felt like an imposter, like I'd snuck in.

I silenced him by overachieving. I threw myself into my classwork and learned to fake confidence during class. I worked so hard there was no space in my mind for his voice.

And then, one day, a clean, white envelope arrived in the mailbox. Gingerly, I slit open the envelope and slid out the single page inside. My breath caught when I read the words: *Congratulations on your admissions to UNR.*

I had been the three-year-old whisked to the park so her father could be carried away in a black bag. I had been the five-year-old sent to a "boarding school" in iFafa. I had been the fourteen-year-old immigrant to an alien country, and for over a decade, I had been burdened with secrets no one should have to carry.

I was twenty years old and ready to leave behind my old identities and set my sights on a new one: a straight-A student at a real American university.

19

IF ON A SATURDAY AFTERNOON IN SEPTEMBER OF 1992, you hovered miles above Earth, and if your eye has grown tired of the late-summer greens and floral abundance of the Eastern seaboard of the United States, or your ear has found monotonous the summer laughter of children playing on the shores of thousands of glittering lakes in the Midwest, you might be drawn to the endless brown of the Western high deserts stretching from Colorado all the way to mid-California, from eastern Washington to the Mexican border. If you found yourself hovering over the vast expanse between Sacramento in the west and Salt Lake City to the east, and if you were to settle onto a hillside at a latitude of 39.5° N and a longitude of 119.8° W, you would find yourself in the desert city of Reno, Nevada.

It is late summer, and the greens and yellows of Reno's grassy hills have turned a dusty brown. Even the buildings have adopted a monochromatic tan. You might be tempted to move from this sterile American desert to the summer adventures of amusement park country to the southeast, or to the primordial innervation of bayou country, but listen carefully, and you will hear something resembling a roar, a churning on the ground, a rising and falling train of sound, voices lifted up in praise.

Football.

College football.

Part religion, part cultural touchstone, part American pastime, part gladiator arena, part skill, part brute strength, part tactical, part luck, part surgical, part blunt instrument, college football is God. And, for the next four years, God lives in Reno, Nevada.

Not surprisingly, the first time I saw him was in the UNR football stadium. I was surrounded by thousands of loyal fans, collectively submerged in the Nevada heat characteristic of September before temperatures drop to the low 70s in October. I had never attended a football game nor even watched one on TV. I was at the stadium only because of Tania. She'd asked me to come with her, insisting again and again that it would be fun, until finally I relented.

Brown hills stretched in every direction beyond the walls of the stadium, where the fans arranged themselves on hot steel benches. They filled the still desert air with cheers, bellowing horns, pitched screams.

The game itself was hard for me to understand, but in truth, I didn't give it more than a few seconds of my time. Instead, my eyes took in everything around me. Blue paint covered the faces of die-hard Wolf Pack fans. There was the dancing wolf mascot itself, the animated cheerleaders, even the advertisements around the stadium shouted their enthusiasm:

Allstate Rental Car Sales—We Support The Pack!!!

Make Us Part of Your Game Plan—Club Cal Neva

Western Nevada Supply Co.—Good Luck Wolf Pack, John Assuages Nugget. News Channel 8.

After I had read every sign and taken in every sight, I began to wish I had brought a book.

I've never appreciated watching any sport as I'm more of a doer than an observer. If Coloured girls in South Africa had been permitted to participate in sports under Apartheid, I might have played something other than the egg and spoon race on sports day. I'm not particularly tall, but I imagine I would have enjoyed being on a swimming or volleyball team. I understand the need for entertainment, but I do not understand the almost religious fervor of die-hard sports fans with respect to their favorite team. Whatever the sport, the outcome is the same. There is always a winner. There is always a loser. There are never real-world consequences. I have no patience for fans who sit in the bleachers or on their couches convinced they could do better than the athletic specimens out on the field as they judge and curse the athletes who are getting their bodies bashed. In reality, most of these fans would not make a sprint around a football field. Instead, they sip/gulp beer, wash down another nacho, and rant and rave as to who on the field should get fired and who should keep their jobs. Should their team win, there is even more beer to be consumed and more to celebrate before they head to their 9-5 jobs to brag about "my team," which won the day before, as if they actually had something to do with it. Meanwhile, the world ticks forward.

Sitting in the smoldering haze of the UNR stadium, I shifted my gaze to the field where the action was supposedly taking place and found myself critiquing the unattractive pants worn by the players. Spandex and men just don't go together, I thought. Marcel had created in me an aversion to clothes drawing suggestive attention to the male form. Whenever he summoned me to rub his back, he would undress in front of me, leaving on just his tight briefs. The players' white uniform pants reminded me too much of what I wanted to forget.

Repellent thoughts of men in spandex fled my mind when my eye was caught by a strikingly tall figure on the field.

Number 75.

Most football players appear to be only slightly smaller than a large hatchback, but this one rose above even his teammates. He had long, muscular legs, a broad torso, and shone from the field like the sun itself.

I couldn't take my eyes away.

His height first caught my eye, but then I was captivated by the way he moved. When he walked, it wasn't with a strut or a shuffle but with long, confident strides. He possessed a beautiful mobility that seemed to flow with an invisible tide. When he returned to the sideline bench and removed his helmet, I saw he had blond hair in a crew cut and fair, flushed-pink skin.

"Tania, who is number 75?"

Between cheers of "Go Wolf Pack!" she shrugged, "I don't know."

I turned my attention back to the player in the royal-blue jersey and might have made it through the entire game just watching him until someone splashed beer onto the bench next to me.

I turned back to Tania, "How much longer is this game?"

Tania had friends across the colour spectrum and had an early attraction to dating Black men. She questioned me one day, somewhat accusatory, how it was so that my two relationships had been with White men.

"Why have you only dated Brian and Dan?"

"What do you mean?"

"They are both White?"

"Should I give them both a prize for being White?"

"No, but how come you have not dated any Black guys?"

"Because Brian and Dan both happened to be good people who I liked."

"That's odd."

"Are you suggesting I am a racist for not dating a Black man?"

"No. It's just odd."

Though I didn't admit it at the time, Tania was right. It was odd. In South Africa, I had only ever been to one White person's house. It was for a farewell *braai* at the house of Marcel's White boss, Mr. Mineer. I never even went inside Mr. Mineer's house, because the *braai* was in his back yard, and that's where I stayed. If the experience taught me anything about White people, it was that I did not identify with them. Even moving to America didn't change that for me. I was Coloured. I am Coloured. Why then have I never dated someone like me?

In hindsight, I believe Marcel's inappropriate sexualization at such a young age created in me a subconscious aversion to men of his colouring. For this reason, I felt most comfortable in an intimate relationship harboring no reminders of this man. Even mustaches and boxer physiques, both pronounced characteristics of Marcel, were also most off-putting. In my more reflective moments, I wonder if there were Marcels in the lives of my great-great-grandmothers that contributed to their attraction to my Welsh and English progenitors. Of course, this begs the question, would I even be here if not for a Marcel from the distant past? And I shudder.

My unconscious propensity for White men wasn't the only issue Tania raised with me.

"My friend thinks you are a snob," she said to me one day.

I was shocked. "What? Me?"

"Yes, you keep to yourself, and you can be cold. She waved to you the other day, and you did not wave back."

Five years ago, I might have dismissed this accusation as ridiculously American. I might have even asserted my South African-ness with a smug "This is who I am like it or not" kind of an attitude, intentionally refusing to engage in the inane rituals of smiling and hugging and waving at every person I met. But I had been in the country too long, and I took note of what Tania said. Besides, I had always thought of myself as a friendly person who smiled and laughed often, though I had to admit I was guilty of living mostly in my head and sometimes failed to notice others around me.

I resolved to go out more and be friendlier, which is how I came to join Tania for my first football game. It is also how, for the second time in a twenty-four-hour period, again at Tania's urging, I found myself at a party that night—an event I was less than thrilled to attend but which would change the trajectory of my life.

20

THE FRAT HOUSE SAT ON A SMALL DIRT HILL ON the fringe of Interstate 80. There were maybe two hundred students inside, spilling out over the balconies of both the front and back yard. Music blared as students danced, though the rooms were too crowded to move in any direction, so the dancing consisted mostly of jumping up and down while cheap beer and wine splashed from plastic cups.

We had come with a mutual friend, Joey, but as the disorder of the party enveloped us, we got separated. I was scanning the crowd, hoping to find an exit, when Tania tapped me on my shoulder. "Hey, there's number 75, the guy you asked about today." She pointed toward the front door. I swung my head around, and there he was: the larger than life figure, now ducking through the door frame to enter the room. Straightening out his giant body, he stood taller than any human I had ever seen. I watched him survey the crowd, his eyes coming to rest in my direction. We saw each other at the same time, and at that moment, the room, the music, the people all became more than props on a stage, something, in a way, to simply navigate. He smiled, revealing dazzling white teeth. I caught myself smiling back before quickly looking away, flustered, but something had been set in motion. We took the first of many steps toward each other.

Before the tall stranger could reach me, however, a voice jolted me back to the party. It was Joey. "There you are! I've been looking for you. Let's go outside."

Joey, a top-heavy football player, had recently shown a keen interest in me. He was solid in stature, determined in nature, and generally pleasant to be around. Though I had no romantic interest in him, had he shown up a minute sooner, I would have been grateful for the excuse to make an exit; the press of people was becoming agonizingly claustrophobic. The appearance of Number 75 had changed the equation, and he was moving toward me. Before I could respond, however, Joey wrapped a muscular arm around my waist and, with a quick pivot, shuffled me through the crowd and out of doors. I spent the next few minutes scanning the sea of people for Number 75, but he had disappeared.

I'M STANDING ON A BALCONY OVERLOOKING THE crowd below. It is nice up here, away from the stumbling drunkenness, the ear-piercing music, the scattered beer bottles, and plastic cups. I breathe in the cool night air.

Behind me, someone says, "Hi!" and for reasons I cannot explain, I know who it is, and I know he is talking to me.

There he is—all 6 feet 8 inches of him, with those broad shoulders and wide smile. Taking in the stillness of the Nevada night air, I wondered how a figure so large could have possibly disappeared. I know his eyes, a deep, prismatic blue, and I know his smile; I've seen it before. This Number 75 smiles from his heart in a way that reminds me of Father.

"I'm Deron. What's your name?"

The corner of my eyes crinkle as my smile grows.

"Gillian."

"Billion?"

"No, Gillian!"

"What kind of a name is Zillion?" he jokes. He radiates a boyish mischievousness that, somehow, makes me feel more playful than I ever felt as a little girl. I had the feeling with him that I was meeting someone

I had known before, someone deeply familiar as if we both spun on the same invisible thread. We spend the rest of the night until the early hours of the morning sitting on a well-worn couch on the frat house balcony. No one else exists for us.

I am laughing easy and hard at something Deron said when a voice from the darkness interrupts us. "Man, where the hell have you been? I've been looking all over for you."

Deron hollers back, "What? You can't give me a ride home?" He turns back to me, "That's my roommate, Scott. He can't give me a ride home." With a sly smile, he adds, "Any chance I can I get a ride home with you?"

Joey has left the party long before, but Tania is still lingering, waiting for me. The three of us walk to my car. Tania and I watch as Deron folds his long body into the back of my two-door 1980 Ford Mustang. His enormous body takes up the entire back seat of the car. His knees skim the roof. Tania gingerly repositions the passenger seat before sliding into the front. I settle into the driver's seat, acutely aware of Deron's presence, inches behind me, and drive off.

IF I WERE INCLINED TO BELIEVE IN DESTINY OR A power that directs the paths of men and women—and how can one ever be certain either way?—then it was God who took me from my mango tree in Greenwood Park and led me to a frat house on a small dirt hill in Reno where Number 75 could find me standing in the dark.

21

DERON RONALD THORP WAS BORN AND RAISED in the bedroom community of Santa Clara in Northern California's South Bay. His father was a police officer and his mother a teacher. They were reserved in their manners, and I forever wondered where Deron got his easy and carefree spirit. He was serious but never mean; playful but never childish. He excelled at sports, his sheer size and strength giving him an edge. Yet, for all his size, he was graceful, not bullish. He had a great aptitude for academics and never had to study much for any test, but he was never frustrated with people who were slower or duller than he was, and he was patient beyond words with people he cared about; he wanted to understand what made them tick. Though Deron knew very little about South Africa, he took the time to know me. Sometimes he would tell me, with his playful confidence, that he knew me better than I knew myself. I know he did.

Shortly after we began dating, Mummy divorced Marcel, and Deron was happy to accompany me on a visit to see her. Around me, Mummy laughs often, because I am usually goofy and joke around a bit, but to those who don't know her, Mummy can appear somewhat reserved. I don't remember which side of Mummy Deron saw on our first visit, but I remember that months later, he encouraged me to get her a dog. He had picked up on her loneliness, and he thought a dog might brighten her mood and bring a good energy to the house. We picked out an active little mutt from the pound, which she named Java.

I moved in a state of continual wonder at Deron's ability to understand others in ways that went beyond the superficial.

DERON PULLS ME UP FROM THE SOFA WHERE I HAVE surrounded myself with a solar system of textbooks, binders, and at least eight different colored pens. Richard Clayderman's Ballade Pour Adeline is playing. "You need balance," Deron says and pops out my CD from the stereo. "And Damn, G, you need to lighten up with the elevator music." He runs a cigar sized finger across the spines of his CD collection. "I'm going to introduce you to some *real* music." He selects one from his collection and looks at it as though it is a delicacy. "Yasss . . . perrrrfect." He inserts it into his stereo (the volume of which is always set to 11):

> *"With so much drama in the L-B-C*
> *It's kinda hard bein Snoop D-O-double-G*
> *But I, somehow, some way*
> *Keep comin' up with funky ass shit like every single day—"*

I gather my jaw from the floor and peel what is left of my eardrums from the walls. "Really? You call this music?" I shout over the din. "How am I supposed to study with this racket?"

"You're not. You're supposed to get your groove on, G."
The windows shake, but whether it is from the thumping
bass or the 300-pound man moving to the beat of Snoop
D-O-double-G, I can't tell.

I watch Deron, laughing, as he nods his head to the
beat, his shoulders and waist threatening to separate
from his torso. He is wearing knee-length khaki shorts,
a T-shirt, and Birkenstocks, and it hits me for the first
time that I am in a relationship with a White man.

FROM OUR FIRST NIGHT TOGETHER AT THAT FRAT
party I had not wanted to attend, I never had to do anything other than be myself with Deron. In him, I found a
place in America where I finally belonged. He embraced
all of me: the African, the White, the broken, the strong,
the frightened, the free spirit, the whole. This wasn't
some illegal fling, but a real relationship—my first real
relationship, in fact, ignoring one or two forgettable liai-
sons in high school. I had come to the US neither understanding nor caring to understand anyone but those of
colour, like me, but in time I gently laid down the chips I
had brought with me from Durban and carried with me
all those years.

One of the final chips Deron helped me lay to rest
was my Rolux Magnum hair.

I had been straightening my hair since I was eight
years old, and I never let anyone see it kinky. Then one
evening, I don't remember the circumstances, Deron

came over before I had had time to straighten it and saw it in its "homeland" state. He loved it.

"G, why do you waste time straightening your hair when it's so awesome natural?"

"You mean you like it curly?"

"Your hair is badass! I've never seen more beautiful hair."

I had certainly received compliments on my hair before, but only in its processed state. Until the age of about seven, my hair was soft and loose. Thereafter, it bloomed into the wild kinky curls that would define me forever. The only man who had ever seen all its kinkiness was Marcel, and until Deron, no one had loved me for it. In return for this gift, I loved Deron back with a love I had only ever given my father.

Deron and I moved in together our sophomore year of college, and Tania secured her own apartment. She still worked at Albertsons, but we saw little of each other. Mummy had divorced Marcel a year prior, and with that last thread to our shared abuse cut, Tania and I drifted even further apart. Thurn still lived with Mummy in the Reno house, so I would see him occasionally when I visited with Deron. Mummy admired Deron greatly and delighted in his playful teasing. My anger toward her had abated since the divorce, so I was able to join in their banter. My only request of her was to change the married name she held from Marcel back to her maiden name. She did.

I suppose this is the point of the story where one expects Mummy, my siblings and I to come together as a family, reunited after years of separation, abuse, and neglect. But we didn't. You may imagine our shared experiences ultimately brought us closer together. I've certainly seen my share of Lifetime movies where that is the case, but it was not the case for us. Mummy remained detached, and Tania, Thurn, and I continued to find protection in disconnection. Friends have asked me, "Don't you feel sad not having a closer relationship with your siblings?" Perhaps. I certainly feel something when I consider how different our lives might have been if Father had never taken his life or if Mummy had never traded us for Marcel. Is that sadness? I'm not sure. Having never had the family my friends imagine I lost, I'm not sure I know what I feel.

One thing I know for sure is that even if it hadn't been Father's death or Mummy's despair to draw us apart, it would have been Apartheid. That was Apartheid's aim: secure power for the White by drawing the non-White apart. Its mistake was in supposing that security would breed strength in Whites, and suffering would breed weakness in everyone else. In fact, Whites, living in their pampered world of Land Rovers, leather shoes, wool socks, frills, and band-aids when they fell, grew entitled and weak while the rest of us, those who survived, grew strong in the knowledge that we had fought for everything we had. Apartheid was inherently unsustainable.

When I turned twenty-one, I secured a job at the Reno Hilton as a cocktail waitress. By this time, Deron and I had known each other for a little over one year. The pay was decent, but the tips were substantial enough to cover all my bills, including tuition. The money I made at the

Hilton was better than at any previous job I had held, but I would only last a year. The required uniform—a little black dress with exposed cleavage, push-up bra, high-heels—and the barrage of sexist comments from patrons left me loathing the job. I was a walking sex object. The final straw was the night I came home to Deron in tears.

"I *hate* my job!"

"What happened?"

"This guy came in tonight and sat in my section. So of course, I went over to ask him what he wanted to drink. When I came back with his order, he had a thousand-dollar chip on the table. I put his drink down, and he asked me my name. I said Gillian. Then he asked if it was my stage name. I told him no and said I was not a showgirl but a waitress and that Gillian was my real name. He then put his index finger on the chip and slid it toward me. He said the chip was mine if I would meet him in his room after work. Can you believe it? I'm *so* sick of this job!"

"Did you get the guy's name?" Deron's voice was hard.

I nodded and reached into my purse and pulled out a business card. It was glossy with a slight sheen and green print. Handing it to Deron, I said, "When I told him I was not interested, he pulled this card out. Said he was leaving early in the morning and if I changed my mind, I would know where to reach him."

Deron reached his long arms out to me and pulled my body close to his. "Two things. You are not working there any longer. Don't bother ever going back there. You don't have to deal with this bullshit."

Great idea, in theory, I didn't want to deal with all the sexist bullshit that came with that job, but what other option did I have? How would I pay for school and rent and everything else?

Deron, as always, had an answer. "Get a job on-campus. It won't pay half as much, but you won't have to deal with crap like you do at the Hilton. An on-campus job should cover rent and living expenses. Don't worry about tuition. Most students have some debt, and we will pay off whatever you owe when we graduate and get real jobs."

I kicked off my high heeled shoes and flopped on the hand-me-down sofa. Slipping my hands under my dress, I pulled off my black nylon stockings. "Okay. That's the first thing. What's the second? You said there were two things."

Deron looked at the card in his hand and, with a mischievous smile, said, "Second, we are going to place a call to old Jimboy tomorrow."

"What?"

"Ol' Jim said he was flying back home early in the morning, right?"

"Yes, why?"

"Oh, let's just say I'm going to teach Jimmy a little lesson."

"Deron, please don't do anything bad and get yourself into trouble."

"G, calm down. You worry too much. Let's go to bed. Tomorrow will be fun. You get to quit your job, and Jim will wish he'd never met you. You'll see."

I remembered the night I'd called Tania's boyfriend and said the same thing. Unlike me, I was sure Deron knew exactly what he was going to do. I was both thrilled and terrified to find out what he had in mind.

I quit the waitress job the next day. That night, Deron placed a call to Jim while I listened in on the other line, the mute button pressed.

As wild as this sounds, Jim had actually written his home number on the back of his business card. When Deron called, a woman answered and asked who was calling.

"A colleague," Deron said. "And might I ask, are you Jim's lovely wife?"

"Yes, thank you. Let me get him for you." When Jim came on the line, the conversation went a little like this:

"Jim, Jim, Jim. Shame. On. You."

"Who is this?"

"Who am *I*? The real question is, who the hell are *you*? Married, offering young college girls money to sleep with you? What part of any of this is okay, Jim? Who the hell raised you? What would your mother say about your behavior? What about your wife? How do you think you made Gillian feel?"

No response. I wondered if Jim had hung up, but Deron continued.

"Jim. Let's get something clear here. I see that you're a bigwig CEO schmuck who is not used to answering to others, but when *I* ask you a question, I expect an answer or I can just have this conversation with your wife. Comprendo Jimmy?"

"Yes. Yes. I understand. You're right. Bad. Bad decision . . . ."

"Thus consulteth the lesson Little Jimmy. Michael Corleone sends his regards. Capisce?"

After the scolding Deron gave Jim, we laughed, quite literally, until tears rolled from our eyes. I was sure Jim would not be making such offers moving forward, or would at least think twice before doing so.

By the week after, I had a desk job at UNR that did not require a little black dress.

I don't recall Deron ever so much as telling a white lie. Even with the "Jimmy" phone call where I can imagine anyone else inventing a persona to threaten Jim and impress his girlfriend, Deron only needed to tell the truth. It was my first relationship where I never had to second-guess intentions or motives. My family loved him the same. We all needed a heavy dose of Deron's accepting and caring personality. With him, there were no mysteries to be solved, no secrets to carry, no brownie points to be earned, tallied, and cashed. He loved me in a way I had yearned for my whole life.

Memories of the care Deron showed me, even in the early years of our relationship, are legion. Two memories, in particular, stand out. In the first, he kept me safe. In the second, he encouraged me to learn. Both memories are deeply personal, but what is especially interesting about them, to me at least, is when I have shared them with others, their telling has never been met with anything more than polite notice. I wonder how you will take them.

There had been a drug-related incidence of violence in our college apartment complex, and Deron said to me one day, "G, I was looking at the syllabus and saw that there is a self-defense class. You should sign up for it next semester." Then he placed a black, palm-sized canister on the counter and said, "I bought you this pepper spray. I want you to keep it on your keychain."

"Thank you, Deron. I shall smite my enemies with these vapors and unleash my wrath and vengeance upon them!" Outwardly I joked, but inside I was ridiculously pleased. He was my real-life Superman.

At another time, Deron and I were sitting at home together, talking—about what I can't remember—when he said to me, and this I remember distinctly, "Since you like art so much, you should take a painting class or maybe ceramics. Take a fun class and explore all your interests."

That is it.

Perhaps you, like others, wonder why these memories should be so important to me. They are mundane, you might think, or they are juvenile. Maybe they are. This does not hurt my feelings. One shouldn't expect memories to mean as much to the hearer as to the teller. However, if I have done them justice in the telling—and how can anyone do justice to matters of the heart?— you understand a little better what Deron meant to me. Most of my life, I had been schooled in what love was *not.* It was not lies. It was not abandonment. It was not self-gratification. It was not chastisement, attacks, and betrayal. Finally, I was learning what love *is.* It is encouragement. It is partnership. It is possibility.

HE SEES ME STARING. "I KNOW YOU LIKE ME. I SEE the way you be laughing and giggling every time I walk by."

"Well, don't be so flattered," I reply. "I laugh at everything."

"You don't laugh at that," he says, nodding toward my homework spread over the couch.

"That's just something I'm supposed to do. I don't have to like it."

He walks over to me. "Yeah, well, I still know you like me."

I laugh. Of course I like him. I like him more than anyone I have ever met. He is my absolute best friend. My protector. My partner.

He moves closer to me and stroking my hair says, "But however much you like me, I like you more." A giant smile spreads across his face. It reminds me of the sun rising.

It must be close to midnight, but I have never seen the sun shine so brightly. The drab brown hills outside glow amber in the dark and the dry night air no longer feels suffocatingly hot. The room is alive with music.

22

NINETEEN-NINETY-SEVEN WAS FILLED WITH wine and some roses. It was the year I became a university graduate. It was the year Deron and I luxuriated on European shores. It was the year he asked me to marry him.

Deron had been scouted and signed the beginning of our senior year, first with the newly-named Baltimore Ravens, and then a better deal with the New York Giants. He graduated early to begin his life as a professional football player, and I had stayed on to finish school.

When I collected my degree from the University of Nevada, Reno, all was better than well. I was a college graduate. I was confident I had silenced the voice that, for years, told me to keep my mouth. I was in love with a man who loved me back and whose dream of playing in the NFL had come true.

During the summers, Deron participated in the World League of American Football, a summer league where younger NFL players could get more game experience during the off-season. When he was assigned to play for the Barcelona Dragons, I joined him in Sitges, Spain: a quaint seaside town about twenty miles outside of Barcelona.

It was the summer of 1997.

After morning practice, we reveled together in the sky, the sun, our youth. We spent the days soaking in the Mediterranean, dining on paella at our favorite restaurant, the *Santa Maria*, and making love in the warm sand under golden sunsets.

"G, I'VE FOUND GOD," DERON ANNOUNCES. WE ARE sitting on our bed in our Hotel Subur room.

"What?" I look at him in disbelief.

"Yes. I have found God." Deron affects an expression of tranquility.

I'm not sure where this is going, but I decide to play along. "Tell me about this finding of God."

Deron looks down at me and says, "He's down the street. Fifth storefront from the corner down the big alley."

I stare back up at him, "God, huh? Storefront, huh?" I roll my eyes.

"Let's go," Deron says. "I'll introduce you. Everyone should meet God." He jumps up and grabs my hand. "Besides," he says, "I'm hungry."

We walk down the street and turn into "the big alley." Five storefronts down, Deron stops and looks with reverential eyes at the storefront. "Ready?"

Apparently, God lives in a sandwich shop. "Suuur-reee," I drawl.

We walk in, and I can't help but look around for a sign of God: a cross, a religious icon, an incense burner. There is nothing, only a small man hovered over a cutting board, slinging meat. He has no hair except a black fringe in the back of his head, and his brow is furrowed in concentration. He doesn't look up.

Deron leans toward me and whispers, "There He is. Sandwich Jesus."

I started laughing.

Deron walks over to the counter. "Sandwich Jesus!" he says. "What's up?" The man still doesn't look up. All his attention is directed at the sandwiches he's putting together. His fingers and hands fly over the bread.

Deron continues, "Sandwich Jesus, I know what you're thinking. How did such a dashing couple from the other side of the world follow the thread of fate to your door? Tell me I'm right."

Sandwich Jesus lifts an eyebrow in response. It's the first he's acknowledged our presence.

Deron takes in the eyebrow raise and nods. "You know, I may have made a mistake," he says. Perhaps you are not Sandwich Jesus. After careful consideration and consulting with my lovely bride, we have decided you will henceforth be known as Sandwich Buddha. Your sandwich zen is inescapable. It smells of olive oil and ham." Deron looks at Sandwich Buddha, who may or may not have lifted the other eyebrow in response.

Deron is quick to reassure him. "Don't be alarmed, Sandwich Buddha. We don't want to rub your stomach for good luck. We just want three bikini sandwiches, two for me and one for her."

Sandwich Buddha stops his work. "Three?" he asks in broken English.

"He speaks," Deron whispers to me in awe. I start laughing so hard I snort. Sandwich Buddha gives me a flat look. I find this hilarious and begin laughing even harder.

"Tres," Deron says, "and, thank you, Sandwich Buddha, Lord Jesus, and all that is holy for your sandwiches."

Still laughing, I'm wondering if I can make it to the street before collapsing to my knees.

After a few such visits, Deron begins referring to the man as the Sandwich Nazi for his refusal to smile.

SITGES WAS A QUAINT SEASIDE TOWN, BUT IT KNEW how to party. After every Saturday football game, most of the players and their significant others joined the locals to take part in the vibrant nightlife scene, bar hopping and dancing until the early morning hours. On Sundays, the proprietor of the Hotel Subur would host lavish dinners for the team at a ranch just outside Sitges. It was at one of these parties I undertook the "full-arm extension" challenge. Deron coined the term for a challenge that involved drinking an entire liter of wine by holding the pitcher close to the mouth and slowly extending it until one's arm was fully extended, by which time the canister was or should be emptied. If I recall correctly, I was the only woman in our group to successfully complete the challenge. Certainly, youthful foolishness, but it felt good to be able to do something even some of Deron's teammates couldn't do. There were lots of reasons to smile.

BEFORE HEADING BACK TO HOTEL SUBUR, DERON and I make our ritual stop by the shop of the Sandwich Nazi. It is Deron's mission to break the man's stony exterior. "Tonight, I'm going to get him to smile," he says.

As the Sandwich Nazi prepares our regular "bikini sandwiches"—crispy toasted bread smothered with butter, Iberico ham, cheese, and oregano—Deron tries to engage him in conversation. "My *amigo*, you are making our sandwiches with love? Right?

"Dude, man, you look like you missed out on love thirty years ago. Come on, man. Get over here and let's hug it out. Come on, man. Show me a smile. Want me to come over there and give you a hug? Fine, I'll just come back and hug you tomorrow, but dude, you know why I like your sandwiches so much? Let me tell you, man. Before I started eating your sandwiches, I was 5′7″ and 120 pounds. I was the size of my lady right here. But look at me *now!* Let me tell you, my *amigo,* the growth has been phenomenal. And I just want to say, *gracias!* I'm thinking we should do a training video together."

No matter what Deron says, the man won't even smile. Deron's patter only seems to add to his cantankerous mood.

We leave the shop with our sandwiches, but no smile from the Sandwich Nazi.

"Maybe he doesn't speak English," I say.

He laughs and shakes his head. "Maybe G, but smiles come in all languages."

It is true. Smiles and genuine warmth follow Deron everywhere else he goes.

Incidentally, when we return in 1999 for another season with the Barcelona Dragons, Deron finally gets the Sandwich Nazi to smile. I have a picture of it.

Our days at Sitges stretch before us like the endless Mediterranean sea. Deron and I spend them strolling the village's narrow cobblestoned streets and admiring the classic Spanish buildings adorned with brightly colored flowers in clay planter boxes. I sip on *descafeinado con leche*. I peek in storefront windows and admire Lladró figurines. Whatever route we take, I always find myself stopping at the same store and admiring a Lladró mermaid in the window. She is the length of my hand and lays on her stomach with her arms crossed in front of her, with her fin flipped in the air behind her. She has a string of flowers wrapped around her neck and another in her flowing hair. Her free and easy smile mesmerizes me.

"If you like it so much, why don't you just get it?" Deron asks.

"No way, it's too expensive," I insist. "I just like looking at it. Like the ocean, I can't take it home, but I can admire it."

SHORTLY AFTER RETURNING FROM OUR SPANISH summer, Deron suggested we plan a hike up to Half Dome's peak. Throughout our years at the University of Nevada Deron and I had spent many weekends hiking and camping in the Sierra Nevadas of Tahoe and Yosemite. Deron was drawn to activities that pushed him to his limits, and because Half Dome challenged him, it became a favorite. For me, I was drawn to the sunsets, which made the hills of Yosemite Valley appear to shine with molten gold.

It had been a while since we'd seen the valley at sunset, and Deron said he needed a good climb. For this reason, we woke at five the next morning and made the three-hour drive to Yosemite.

AS WE CLIMB, WE PASS A FELLOW HIKER WHO ASKS where we are headed. Deron tells him we are hoping to catch the sunset. The hiker nods, then, almost as an aside, mentions that Glacier Point is the place to see the most magnificent sunsets over Yosemite Valley. We thank him for the tip, and I say something noncommittal like, "We'll definitely have to check it out sometime," but now Deron wants us to hike to Glacier Point, not Half Dome, by sunset. I argue that it's too far, we won't make it, how do we even know it will be better, but once Deron has his mind made up on something, there is no changing it.

We adjust course for Glacier Point.

Deron always hikes with long strides equaling at least three of mine, but now that we have to make Glacier Point by sunset, he climbs even more quickly. I follow in his size 16 footsteps, huffing and puffing after him, as we clamber over steep grade and exposed rocks.

"Slow down Deron. I can't keep up."

"Nah, you're doing great!"

"Why are you in such a hurry today?"

"Just trying to get a good workout in."

"Great for you, but I'm dying back here!"

"Don't you want to see the sunset? I know how you love sunsets."

"I would have been just fine seeing it from Half Dome, thank you."

Though I am slightly perturbed at our frenzied pace, I've become accustomed to keeping up with a professional athlete. The truth is, irritated or not, I would happily follow him up any mountain.

We reach Glacier Point before sunset, my aching legs feeling less like limbs and more like a pair of dull weights. We've been hiking since the crack of dawn, at a speed that felt inhuman, and as I sprawl across the warm rock, giving thanks to the sheltering sky for getting through today's adventure, there is not a soul who could convince me to take another step—not even Deron.

I douse my face with a bottle of water and wipe the sweat with the T-shirt I am wearing. The water revives me slightly, enough for me to take a deep breath and roll into a sitting position. Sitting on a rock, I take in the staggering beauty of Yosemite's grand valley. An August sunset painted the sky; it is, I have to admit, a magnificent place to take in the view. Suddenly, Deron is in front of me on bended knee.

"Will you marry me?" His smile stretches as wide as Glacier Point.

I've known this was coming at some point. If I'm honest, I've known, in a way both magical and strange, since the first moment I saw him, towering above his teammates at the UNR stadium, but the reality of it hits me in a way I never imagined. This is real, I tell myself. This is happening.

Yes, I say to him, yes. A thousand times, yes.

We sit, smiling at the view, sipping wine Deron had hidden in his backpack. He whispers to me that he'd contemplated proposing in Spain, and had even searched for a ring. "But," he laughs, "I wasn't sure of the quality of their diamonds, and I didn't want to end up with a cubic zirconia when we got home." Then he reaches back into his pack and pulls out one more surprise: the smiling Lladró mermaid.

23

"Breathe in, breathe out. Without the fire, the phoenix never rises from the ashes. Let the fire scorch the skin and burn the soul, allowing yourself to absorb the pain and understand the sincerity of the pain."
—Forrest Burran

HAVE A TRIANGLE-SHAPED SCAR THE SIZE OF A quarter on my left thigh. It marks where I fell in my race up the mango tree. The scar is flesh-colored, bordered by a ragged perimeter, and a thickness uncharacteristic of the rest of the skin on my leg. Those with scars born of similar childhood traumas will understand me when I say that the triangular patch of skin is both more and less sensitive than the surrounding skin. Most of the time, I forget the scar is there, but occasionally, something will brush up against it, and I will feel a slight twinge.

Scars, like memories, have a way of reminding you they're there, whether you care to be reminded or not.

It was spring 1998. Deron had signed with the Giants and would be leaving for New Jersey in two days. I would join him in three weeks, but until then, I was staying with Mummy. We were to be married that summer. It was our last night together, and thanks to a teammate of Deron's who had gotten us a suite, we were spending it at the Eldorado Resort Casino. "We're gonna leave Reno in style," Deron said.

WALKING INTO THE SUITE, I HAVE THE SENSATION that the walls are closing in around me. It is one of the biggest rooms I have ever seen in my life, yet it feels intensely suffocating. Deron must notice something is wrong because he asks if I am okay. I make a joke of it. "Yes, I just feel a little overwhelmed by this fancy room." After a restless night, I am relieved to check out of the Eldorado. *Maybe I am just not used to such fancy arrangements.*

At the airport, I hold onto Deron's giant body, my arms only making it halfway around his torso. This is usual, but the uneasiness I've carried with me from the Eldorado is not. I do not want to let him go. "It's only three weeks," Deron reassures me. I force a smile. Sensing my sadness, he jokes, "I know you like me. I see the way you be laughing and giggling." This playful line of his usually makes me laugh, but the best I could do is force another smile. The strange feeling in me sharpens.

I'm dragging my luggage through the front door of Mummy's house when the suffocation I felt entering our suite at the Eldorado hits me with the force of a punch to my diaphragm. I can hardly breathe. My heart gallops in my chest. I rush outside, thinking I just need some fresh air, but with each inhale, the suffocating feeling intensifies, my heart palpitations increase, and the trembling begins.

I go back into the house, thinking maybe a shower will calm me down and ease the pressure on my chest. I close the bathroom door behind me then lock it. I turn on the water in the shower tub combo. Before I undress, I check the lock again. I check it a third time. I inspect the door for holes. When I find none, I slip out of my clothing and step under the water. I cling to the wall of the bath. I've never seen these tiles from a distance of five inches before. The water pelting my naked body makes it nearly impossible for me to stand. Slowly, I slide to the bathtub floor and lie there, howling.

My chest aches terribly, but I have no idea why. Grief engulfs my body like the waves at Umhlanga Rocks. The water feels suddenly ice cold. My lungs burn for air. I am certain I will drown in this bathtub closing in on me like a monstrous caul.

Somehow, just as at Umhlanga Rocks, I manage to pull myself out of the water. Frantically, I grab for the shower knob, shut off the water and force myself into a seated position. I sit there. Wet and panicked and utterly bewildered.

I am a college graduate with a degree in psychology. I am the first in my family to hold such a distinction. I put a stop to the Marcel show, banishing him from my life, the life of Tania, and of Thurn and Mummy. Why am I falling apart? Was this what happened with Father?

I can't stop the tears. I am terrified because it feels like I am no longer in control. I wrap a towel around my quivering body and watch my feet as they make their way to my old room, the room Tania and I shared until we left. The towel slips off. I don't bend to pick it up. I flop onto the bed and wrap the top cover over myself to help quiet my shaking.

Mummy enters the room. She must have heard me sobbing. She sits at the edge of the bed. I can see the concern in her face.

"Is this how it began for him?" I ask.

What I want to hear is, no, absolutely not. You are different. Nothing like him. Instead, she says, "I don't remember. Let me get you something to eat." She stands up from the bed. "I'll be right back."

Her response only adds to my anxiety. Food is not the comfort I am looking for.

She returns shortly with the best she can do: two fried eggs, two slices of white bread smothered in chunks of butter, and fresh-cut tomatoes speckled with salt and pepper. I begin sobbing again. Mummy repositions herself at the edge of my bed and stares at the ground. After a few minutes, she says in a low voice, "It will be okay." These words are more of a reassurance to Mummy.

"Anxiety is normal for many recent college graduates," Dr. William says as he scribbles out a prescription for anti-anxiety medication. "No job yet, loans, leaving your home of the past four years—the real world awaits. Totally understandable. I see it all the time. Take these, but I also recommend that you see a counselor to talk about some of what you are feeling."

"But I graduated a year ago," I remind him. "Why now?"

He smiles and guides me out of the examination room, past the worn magazines and the plastic potted plants and into the outer office.

"All of this is normal," he says. "In time, it will pass."

None of it feels normal to me. My hands shake as I fumble for my keys, the prescription clutched in one hand. I've been anxious before, but this is something else. I'd tried to convey that to the doctor, but he seemed sure it was perfectly normal. Despite his reassurance, I leave his office more anxious than I'd been when I entered.

I've dealt with the death of my father and a childhood of being shuttled from caretaker to caretaker. I've dealt with an abusive stepfather, years of secrecy, with uprooting my entire life and moving across the world. I've handled being objectified while serving drinks as a cocktail waitress at Reno casinos and managed college just fine with its intense studying and test deadlines. Why am I breaking now? How is it possible to go so suddenly from being perfectly happy to holding a prescription for a psychiatric drug in my jittery hands?

"Keep it together, Gillian," I tell myself as I fumble for my keys.

I am parked in the driveway at Mummy's house and crying uncontrollably. The fleeting sense of dread I felt at Eldorado has blossomed into a nightmare. I've been crying uncontrollably for hours. I should want to get out of this car and go inside, but I can't. It's as if I have been sucked into the drainpipe of Mummy's tub with the water that had swirled around me. I want to run, but where can I run to, and once I get there, then what? Deron is on the other side of the country with the New York Giants. I'm supposed to join him in three weeks, but I question whether I can survive until then.

The thought of being victim to the same urges my father succumbed to fuel my panic. Am I becoming one of the people I had studied during my years of psychology classes and field internships—the very people I am supposed to help? What else can explain all of this? The medication I've been prescribed seems like the best approach to dealing with whatever this is, but I can't stop thinking that Father had taken medication, too.

I've read about such things in school: people falling apart, anxiety, depression, post-traumatic stress disorder. I diagnosed fictional people for reports but never imagined I might have to diagnose myself. I am different from the weeping, wailing, angry, or submissive people around me. I knew how to keep my emotions in check, and I was proud of it.

I stumble from the car, shakily jam my key into the front door to Mummy's house and walk inside. It is the same house we'd lived in when we moved to Reno. It is the house with the fireplace that was put to use in the winter months. It is the house that Mummy once shared with Marcel. It is the house I was told to get out of.

24

WHEN I WAS YOUNG AND LIVING IN SOUTH Africa, I had a recurring dream about waking and finding myself all alone in a house I had never lived in. It was a two-story home. I knew it was a two-story home not from the outside of the house—I never saw the whole house in my dream—but as I always found myself in the same dining room with a staircase. The steps I took in this dream were cold and heavy. The sense of loneliness, terrifying, and I knew I was the only person left in the world. It was the only dream I ever had in black and white.

STILL SHAKING, I RUN TO THE PHONE AND DIAL Deron's number.

"What up, G?" His voice is upbeat, as always. "I can't wait for you to come out here, you're going to love it!"

I immediately begin to cry. It is the only thing I seem to do well any more.

"What's going on? Are you okay?"

Between sobs and deep breaths, I manage to get out, "No, I think—I think I'm going crazy."

"Okay, calm down, G. Take a deep breath and tell me what's going on."

Deron has a way of calming me. He never shows any stress and takes every situation in his stride. "I'm here for you. Just breathe," he says. "Now tell me, what's going on?"

I explain what the doctor said. "But Deron, I think I'm having a nervous breakdown or something of the sorts. No. Actually, I'm going crazy."

"You are *not* going crazy," he assures me, playing the role of the rational side of my brain. "The doctor's right, you're just going through post-graduation anxiety." His voice is even and calm. "There are so many changes going on in our lives right now, and what you're feeling is normal. But you're going to be better than fine because you're stronger than any person I know. And I'm not going anywhere. Our lives are just beginning." He continues, "Just hang in there for three weeks and, in the meantime, make an appointment to see a counselor who can help you while I'm not there."

I agree, and Deron promises he will call me daily.

"Remember, I love you, and I'm by your side even though I'm in New Jersey!"

I hang up, comforted by his words, but it fades in seconds. As soon as his voice isn't in my ear, another wave of anxiety hits me. My hands begin to sweat; my heart races; I become convinced that my throat is closing. I want to run again, but there is nowhere to go. I start crying again.

"Where are you currently staying?" the counselor asks.

"At my mother's house."

"I see. Has anything ever happened to you there?"

All the doors burst open at once, and the ghosts flood into the corridors.

The East Coast

25

THIS PERIOD OF MY LIFE MARKED THE BEGINning of what would later be diagnosed as Post-Traumatic Stress Disorder. PTSD is a mental health condition triggered by a terror-stricken event—either experiencing it or witnessing it. Symptoms are varied, but in my case it left me with nightmares, panic attacks, severe anxiety, and physical sensations such as pain, sweating, nausea, and trembling. PTSD can be triggered months or even years after the event, subjecting sufferers to a debilitating onslaught of disturbing thoughts and feelings related to their experience. It can feel as if one is being pulled between the past and the present.

My whole life, I had protected myself by keeping busy. In college, I would wake at four a.m. for my job at UPS unloading heavy packages. Four hours later, my skin coated in dust, I returned home to take a cat shower, then I was off again to a carefully selected schedule of classes, followed by homework, then evening and weekend shifts at Albertsons. I always tested the limits of how much I could take on, filling every corner of my life with self-imposed challenges: How fast could I check out a full grocery cart? How many more customers could I get through over all the other checkers? What was the maximum amount of courses I could take in a semester? How quickly could I unload a UPS trailer? I took on every challenge I saw in life, even when they would do me nor anyone else any good, from that ridiculous full-arm extension in Spain, to quitting coffee for a year just to prove a point to Deron, to staying at UPS for a year only to show the other workers that I could.

Preoccupation was my protection. It kept all those doors in my mind closed because once closed, what was behind those doors became another person's story. Not mine. I had other things to focus on.

By some miracle I made it to New Jersey. Stepping off the plane, I felt more broken than I ever had in my life. It was as though, once again, I had been robbed of some essential part. The thing I had lost was intangible and of no value to anyone, but I could not survive without it. It was the invisible tether that had been holding me together since Father failed us all with a car filled with odorless, colorless gas.

The medication I was taking only made everything cloudier, creating foggy days blending into sleepless nights. The only feeling I had was in my head: that of a rubber band being pulled and pulled, ready to snap at any moment.

Deron was there to meet me at Newark Liberty International Airport. I don't remember anything of the drive from the airport to the apartment he'd secured for us in Wayne, New Jersey, a moderate-sized one-bedroom rental. Even the furniture was rented. The walls were clean and bare, offering nothing in the way of inspiration. The king-sized bed was comfortable but not long enough to keep Deron's legs from dangling off the end. The apartment complex sat on well-manicured grounds. Everything about the world around me proclaimed simplicity and order. But the fuzziness in my head had seeped out and was blurring everything I saw. I remember staring at a tree outside the window of our apartment, trying to comprehend why it didn't look green. In my psychology classes, I'd learned that color is correlated to emotion: when you are depressed, so too are the colors around you. Just a few short weeks ago, I'd felt joy and seen vibrant colors. Now I was staring at a tree the color of dust, and green was just a memory.

I had never before experienced depression. To my knowledge, neither had Thurn or Tania. In our darkest hours, despite all evidence to the contrary, we had held on to the belief that the world would make sense again. Now, I only felt dead inside. This unfamiliar emptiness terrified me.

Deron had made arrangements for me to see a therapist as soon as I arrived. "We have an appointment with Dr. Roberta tomorrow," he said. He pronounced it "Roww-ber-ta," drawing out the sounds to make me smile.

But I had no energy left to smile. All I could muster was a dull thank you.

ROBERTA HAS AN AURA OF HEALING ABOUT HER. Her hair is cut short to her ears, black with a little grey peppered in it. She appears to be a genuine person who sincerely wants to help people. When she says she is, in fact, a hypnotherapist, I am taken aback, any hope of healing snuffed in disappointment. I want no part of this "voodoo stuff." Still, I remain polite and don't say anything. I remind myself that Deron did his homework. I remind myself he interviewed a number of therapists and chose the one he thought best for me, and that I trust his judgment. I try to keep an open mind, to remember that I am doing this not only for me but for him.

I initially fight Roberta's voice, afraid that if I give in, I will be put into some hypnotic sleep where she will hold control over me. But, as my resistance slowly crumbles, I realize my fears are unfounded. Her voice speaks to me through the walls I've put up, without rupturing them. I find myself in a relaxed, trance-like state, fully aware of my surroundings but deeply focused on her voice. As I lie on the couch, eyes closed, Roberta asks me to go back to my earliest memory.

I'M THREE YEARS OLD, STANDING IN THE LIVING room of our house on Barnes Road. The walls are washed a dull hue from the light hanging from the middle of the ceiling. I am all alone. The sense of loneliness is terrifying, and I wonder where everyone is. Something is wrong, though, because I know Father is here. His presence is so strong, so real, and it fills me with a deep, heartsick longing.

DRIVING HOME THAT EVENING, I TOLD DERON I didn't know if hypnotherapy was for me. "I don't want to remember this stuff, Deron," I said. "I want nothing more than to just forget everything."

He tells me to be patient and give it another try. He thinks Roberta is going to help me. He *knows* she is. Maybe she is, but I'm not convinced help has to hurt this much.

I told him I had been thinking about electroconvulsive shock therapy.

Deron laughed. "Are you really serious?"

"Very. We learned about it in one of my psychology classes, and one of the side effects is memory loss. I'm thinking it might be a better therapeutic option for me." I began to cry. "It was as though I were back there, Deron," I said. "The picture was so clear. It was like I *was* that little girl again: scared, lonely. I'm three years old, standing in the living room of our old house on Barnes Road. The light's on—it's not very bright, and walls are off-white. I'm the only person in the house, and I have this paralyzing fear I've been abandoned. I'm not crying. Just terrified and wondering why they left me."

I cried all the way home. I continued to cry as we walked through our apartment door. Deron held me in his arms and guided me to the living room couch. He held me while I cried until nothing was left in me. Then, he carried me to bed.

I WAKE IN THE EARLY HOURS OF THE MORNING, pushing and kicking the covers off my body. I try to scream, but nothing comes out.

"You're safe now," Deron says. He's holding me in his arms.

"NO! Get away—get away!" I struggle to break free, but he holds on.

I come back to myself, but I am still shaken, frantic. "He was here! Lying next to me! And he put his hands under my clothes!" Deron holds me in his strong arms as I continue. "I ran to the closet, and I was tying my pants back tight, and he said, 'Do you really think you can get away from me?' He was coming closer and reaching his hand out, and I tried to scream to let you know he was here, but nothing would come out." I'm shaking, feeling physically and mentally drenched.

"That's your past," Deron says. His voice calms me, as always. "You're remembering your past, but you're safe now. I'm here, and you don't have to be afraid anymore. He will never hurt you ever again. I won't let him."

My waking panic has passed. Deron's words reassure me, and I allow myself to be cradled in his arms until I fall asleep again.

I wake feeling beat-up and groggy. It's morning, but I don't know what time. I assume Deron has left for football practice. I am alone in the apartment. I shuffle to the bathroom. Swollen eyes and a puffy face look back at me from the mirror. A note from Deron sits on the bathroom counter, but I have little strength or interest in reading it. I leave it where it sits and slowly shuffle back to the bedroom, where I stare out the window at a flock of crows.

IN THE WEEKS SINCE I'D SAT CRYING IN MY mother's bathtub, my depression had deepened dramatically. It became so dark, it blacked out all the light in me. Every waking minute, every simple task—brushing my teeth, checking the mail, smiling at Deron when he returns home—felt impossible. I spent hours looking at the crows that flocked and screeched outside our window. If someone had asked me what I was thinking, I might have answered that I wanted to be one of those birds and fly out of the prison I found myself in. What I really wanted was to die.

In my second session with Roberta, I told her about the overwhelming despair I felt. To my surprise, she said she would refer me to Dr. Doller, a psychiatrist in White Plains, New York. "I think it will be helpful if you go on an antidepressant medication to help you cope while we work together on your path to healing," she said. I said nothing and politely took the referral she sent me home with, but I had no intention of going to another doctor or taking more pills.

A few days later, spurred by wrenching dreams and hopeless mornings, I visited Dr. Doller, who prescribed me the medication.

"What if these pills make me hear voices?" I asked. I remembered Mummy saying that Father started hearing voices after he went on his medication.

"Just look at these pills as 'floaters,'" Dr. Doller said simply, "They'll keep you afloat as you paddle your way to shore."

I BEGIN TO THINK THAT MY ANTIDEPRESSANTS might serve as a way out. Deron deserves more than I can give him. Whatever had kept me tethered is gone. I am broken and have drifted to a place so dark I will never find my way back. I am just taking up space. I am useless. I know of only one way this medicine can fix me.

I find myself once again staring at the crows through our bedroom window. In my desperate fog, their sharp caws beckon to me. It is so simple: Deron and I can both be free—he to follow his passion without a broken-down fiancée and me to leave behind the chaos and ghosts and the utter blackness I'm buried in. Death is my lifeline. I don't know precisely what it is, but I know I need it. It will be my new gravity. If Father could have made such a decision, then perhaps I can, too. I can escape.

When Deron gets home, I am still in my pajamas.

"Why don't you change, and let's go out tonight," he says.

"Deron, please let me go."

"What are you talking about?"

I haven't moved from my perch in front of the window. I alternate between looking at him and looking out the window. The crows have flown.

"This is it for me," I say. "You have done more for me than anybody on this Earth, and I love you for that, but you deserve more than I can give you. Please. Let me go."

"Go where?"

"If I stay, I'm going to end up in a mental institution. But you have so much ahead of you. It's best if we go our separate ways."

He looks directly into my eyes, and in a firm voice, he says, "You aren't going anywhere." He continues, "And if you do end up in a mental institution, I will be right there by your side. I am never leaving you, G. We can go crazy together."

I HAD ALWAYS THOUGHT OF EARTH AS A CONSTANT: the literal rock upon which all manner of beasts moved, mother of vast oceans, keeper of secrets thousands of miles deep, the densest planet in our solar system. Then something untethered me from gravity, and I began to drift in ways and to places I didn't know were possible. Earth ceased to matter, and life became a dull abstraction. I can never really know whether that something was the shower at Mummy's house, the night at Eldorado, or the morning I woke and discovered that Father, the man I thought I would marry, had failed our family. Whatever it was doesn't matter, because when it happened, I had Deron. He was my protector, my partner, the man who brought color back into my life, and on July 11, 1998, not even a month after my twenty-seventh birthday, I married the man I knew would never, ever, fail me.

26

DURING THAT SUMMER OF 1998 ON THE EAST Coast, with love as the driver and Roberta as the navigator, I found myself on the road to recovery. Deron drove me to see Roberta every week, and I diligently did her assigned homework: reading books, journaling, taking daily walks, meditating. I was a good student, and though I didn't know if these things would make any difference, I persisted. I kept busy between counseling sessions with temporary jobs and genuine, but futile attempts to connect with the other football players' wives in the NFL Players' Wives Association. Deron and I had moved to Long Island, where the lament of mourning doves replaced the wintry screech of crows. On especially dreary days when mist threatened to choke the island, the fog horns would cut through the haze. It was a lonely but hopeful sound.

DERON AND I ARE WALKING ALONG THE BEACH near our home in Long Island, when apropos of nothing he turns to me and says, "Welcome back!"

"What? What do you mean?"

"We've been talking about politics for the past thirty minutes. I haven't heard you talk about politics since college."

The sand at our feet glimmers white, and to our left, the ocean reflects the blue sky above. Deron is right. Through the grey, I am beginning to see slices of light.

MUMMY EMBRACED DERON AS A MEMBER OF THE family as well as she had ever been able to embrace anyone since Father's death. Deron loved Mummy, despite her faults, and he affectionately nicknamed her Mumalini. He delighted in her easy-going manner and ability to cook spicy dishes. The first time Deron had my mother's lamb curry was in the dead of a Reno winter, and he ran outside into a storm, red-faced, sweat dripping from him and shoved snow into his mouth to quell the heat. Watching him through the dining room window, we laughed at this American guy who had never in his life been exposed to spicy food. Returning inside, Deron said brightly, "Mumalini, that stuff is good. Is there any more?"

When Mummy was young, she had been beautiful enough to be crowned Miss Sydenham, three times. Although she is no longer the shiny and bright sunbeam I remembered from childhood, she was still beautiful to me. My experience with PTSD had softened any lingering bitterness I might have felt toward her, and now I not only love her but appreciate her. We still lived thousands of miles apart but kept in touch over regular phone calls.

It was during one of these calls that Mummy told me that my cousin Adele, Aunt Myrtle's adopted daughter, had recently moved to New York from South Africa.

Aunt Myrtle was Mummy's older sister and had married a certain Errol Cattell, despite Granny's strenuous objections. Granny so opposed the union she ended up in the hospital the day of Myrtle's wedding as protest. No one remembers what mysterious illness put her there, not even Granny, but whatever it was, she recovered the next day. Myrtle and Errol had four children and adopted a fifth child, named Adele. All their biological children—Andre, Donavan, Jill, and Mark—were varied shades of brown and had distinctly non-White features; Adele, however, had fair skin and except for the dark brown kinky hair might have passed for White.

Adele's nickname was "Mousy," because she was a shy and timid child who behaved as though she were a barely tolerated guest. I remember secretly examining my new cousin from across the room, at one of the family parties at Greenwood Park when I was about eight or nine years old. Even though she was only about five and barely spoke, I saw something familiar in her eyes. Maybe it was yearning. I don't know how old she was when Myrtle and Errol adopted her, but perhaps she knew she had once been someone else's little girl, just as I had been. Perhaps, like me, she wished for the parents she'd lost to come save her from the life she'd landed in.

When I told Deron about Adele living just an hour or so west of us, he suggested we go into the city next week and visit her. "With all you've gone through," he said, "it would be great for you to see family. She's also probably lonely without family around. It will be good for both of you to connect."

I immediately called Aunty Myrtle, who gave me Adele's new address. The following weekend, Deron and I drove to her apartment for a surprise visit.

We arrived, and I pressed the doorbell of Adele's apartment. I listened with eager anticipation to the sound of footsteps moving toward the door. The door creaked open slowly, almost timidly. I recognized her immediately. When she realized it was me, she seemed more shocked than surprised and blurted out, "What are you doing here?" I introduced her to Deron, told her I'd found out about her move from Mummy and that we'd driven over from Long Island to see her. After a brief exchange of pleasantries, the three of us went out for coffee. There was a bit of awkwardness in our meeting, and I found myself surprised that Adele wasn't as excited to see me as I was to see her. Still, we chatted for about an hour before she said she had to leave and get ready for work. We exchanged phone numbers and promised to keep in touch.

It was nice but not quite the reception I had expected.

IT IS A HOT INDIAN SUMMER AFTERNOON, ONLY five days from October with temperatures in the 80s as we leave New York City heading to our rental home in Long Island. Driving back, Deron is unusually quiet.

"Are you okay?" I ask.

"Yeah, I'm just thinking."

"About what?"

"Did you say Adele was adopted outside your family?"

"Yes. I don't know her whole story, but my Aunty Myrtle—my mother's sister—adopted her when she was a baby."

"Hmm."

"What do you mean, hmm?"

"G, you know I never keep anything from you, so I'm going to tell you what's on my mind." His voice is tight. Serious even.

I can't imagine what's on his mind, but it sure has him behaving strangely.

He continues. "There is no way Adele was adopted from outside of your family."

Whatever I might have thought he was going to say, it wasn't this. I'm utterly confused. How can someone be adopted but still be born in the family? It's like Father's saying about looking at the sky and looking away from it at the same time. I can't make sense of it. "What on earth are you talking about, Deron?"

"Did you not see what I saw today?" Deron looks over at me, his bright blue eyes insistent, but careful. It's as if he's measuring my reaction, or perhaps my strength. He must see something reassuring him, because he continues: "She looks like your sister, G. Actually, you look like you could be twins."

For some reason, this annoys me, and I turn on him. "You're talking absolute nonsense, Deron! We don't look at all alike." I pull out my phone. Now I'm indignant. "I'm going to call Aunty Val right now—you'll see, Adele is my *adopted* cousin." I dial Aunty Val's number. She picks up almost immediately. When I tell her why I'm calling and ask if she knows who Adele's biological parents are, she says, "You mean you still don't know?"

"Don't know what?"

After a pause, she says, "Adele is your sister, Gillian."

I am dumbfounded.

"Hello? Gillian, are you there?"

"I'm here," I reply flatly.

There's another pause. "Are you okay?"

I reassure her that I am fine, thank her for the information and end the call. Deron is silent in the seat next to me.

This can't be happening. Just as I was coming out of the grey, beginning to piece things back together, I learn of a sister who was raised as my cousin. *What kind of bladdy family was I born into?* It's almost too ridiculous for words. What's next? Uncle Johnny is really Mummy's brother? I am angry. No. Anger is an understatement. I am outraged. *Who the fuck are these people?*

27

ADELE HAD KNOWN SHE WAS MY SISTER FROM when she was very young. She wasn't even ten years old when she had stumbled upon her birth certificate with my mother's name on it: Lorraine August.

Mummy had hidden the pregnancy well. A few months after Thurn, Tania and I were sent to live with Granny and Uncle Johnny, those close to her noticed that she had begun to gain weight. Everyone, even Granny, believed it was out of grief over Father's death. At a party one night, Mummy said she was sick and was rushed to the emergency room. Someone must have called Granny. Granny, who had already had one child taken from her and who had just lost her son-in-law, must have thought she was about to lose another daughter. I can't imagine the fear and the worry she must have felt as she drove to the hospital. I wonder if she thought of her father-less grandchildren and prayed they would not lose their mother, too.

When Granny found out the truth, I don't know if she took it with relief, outrage, or resignation. The father, she would learn, was a man named Carl, one of Father's good friends. It must have happened shortly after Father's death; I imagine a tryst born out of mutual loneliness and pain. I imagine weeks, if not months, of invented love, both of them using the other to keep alive a man who had chosen to die.

When Carl realized Mummy was pregnant, did he entertain the notion of stepping into the void left by his friend? If he had, would Mummy have swept back to Granny's and whisked us home? Was it Carl or Mummy who first saw their relationship for the make-believe it was?

Mummy and I do not speak of this time, so I will never know. It is enough for me to know why we were kept at Granny's for as long as we were. Mummy had ghosts of her own she was fighting.

After my call with Aunty Val, I reached out to Adele. I desperately wanted to process this latest revelation with her, but she had no interest in speaking with me. "I was disowned by your mother," she said. "I've been the dirty little secret of the family my whole life, and now that I've come to terms with it, I want to keep separate from all of you."

I was heartbroken, but I also understood. I had seen it at the party in Greenwood Park. We both yearned for something we could never have because of the choices of others. Now that we were in a position to make choices of our own, we could either spend a lifetime wishing that things had been different or learn from the mistakes of others and give ourselves the life we deserved. After years of feeling like a barely tolerated guest in our family, Adele deserved a life of her own. All we truly have in life are our choices, so I left Adele to hers.

I PULL MY HAIR BACK AND WASH MY FACE.

I'm at home alone. Deron is out playing a game of basketball and hanging out with friends for the day. It's a bright spring day, and I have nothing else planned except writing my letter to Marcel. It will be my closure letter. I have talked it through with Deron for about a week, and now I'm ready to begin.

I dry my face with my bathrobe, grab the laptop, and head outside to a bench on the front porch of our home, which I have previously designated as the setting for my letter.

I type. I laugh. I type. I cry. I type. I scream. I type. I type. I stop. I breathe. I pace. I type.

I type.

I type.

I type.

The June sun warms the Santa Clara breezes that occasionally gust through my hair.

Light and shadow dance past, marking time as day marches silently into night.

IT'S BEEN ALMOST TWENTY YEARS SINCE I WROTE that letter. It is five pages long. I kept a copy which I cringe now to read. It opens with a catchy, "You are probably wondering why I have taken the time out to write this letter . . ." then gets right to the point by demanding Marcel, "let me get to the point." It details every abuse my family and I experienced at Marcel's hands.

I knew, when I wrote it, that I was going to send a copy to Marcel, and I entertained extensive fantasies of what he might do when he received it. I imagined him seized with impotent rage, wanting to destroy me but powerless to do so. I imagined him throwing the letter away, or tearing it up, or crumpling it to the ground, thinking that would be enough to silence me. But no matter what he did, the letter was picked up off the floor, pieced back together, or dug out of the trash. In every fantasy, he was compelled to read every single word.

In reality, I knew there was a good chance Marcel would not finish it. After all, the letter was over 2,000 words, and I'm not sure he even knows two hundred, so I wrote it in a way that would be impossible for him to miss the point.

Throughout the letter, I engaged ALL CAPS, Title Case, and the **bold function** to the extent that even a casual reader with only a few minutes to spare could not fail to get the main idea:

> *I Don't like you; I NEVER have and NEVER will. . . .*
> *"PIECE OF SHIT," . . . "SCUM OF THE EARTH," . . .*
> *"FUCKER," . . . REALLY IS . . . Did You Have No*
> *Mercy??? . . .* ***you sickened me more than you will***
> ***ever know*** *. . . No!!!!! Well FUCK YOU and FUCK*
> *the apology I never received. . . .* ***Pathological Child***
> ***Abuser*** *. . .* ***NEVER*** *Forgive You!!! . . . My Destiny*
> *. . . EVER . . .* ***STOP!!!*** *. . .* ***NOTHING*** *. . .* ***Fortu-***
> ***nately, You Failed Miserably.***

> *Signed,*
> *Gillian Thorp*

My closure letter to Marcel is neither a refined, nor an elegant piece of prose, but I am immeasurably proud of it for at least three reasons.

First, I wrote it.

Second, I sent it.

Third, Marcel's new wife got the first copy.

I mailed the letter to a former UNR teammate of Deron's who still lived in Reno and had agreed to hand-deliver it for me. Marcel had remarried, and when Lamont arrived, his wife answered the door.

"This letter is for you," he said and handed it to her. Then he walked away. I had been very specific in my instructions: I wanted to make sure Marcel's wife got a copy, and that Marcel did not intercept it. I also mailed a copy to his machine shop, and to every family member, on his side and mine. This letter was not only about confronting my abuser; it fulfilled a deep responsibility I felt for any child who might find him or herself in Marcel's company. I ended the letter with a warning that "both Deron and I know many people and we are watching you."

The last line in the letter was a lie: Deron and I had never spied on him, nor did we have connections to "many people" however you wish to interpret that phrase. The purpose of the threat was to scare Marcel into having second thoughts about ever hurting another child.

Santa Clara, California

28

DERON'S FOOTBALL CAREER WAS EXCITING, but after three years of living out of a suitcase, I was done with the instability. I'd had quite enough of that in my life already. While Deron transferred from the Giants to the Jets and then signed with the Detroit Lions, I decided to claim some agency in my life. I returned to the West Coast and enrolled in Santa Clara University's Graduate Counseling Program. We were apart, but we wouldn't be for long.

Shortly after I entered graduate school, Deron was released by the Lions and joined me in California, where he embarked on his own educational journey: enrolling in business school at San Jose State University. We were ready for a stable, steady existence—one involving children—but first, we wanted to share one last adventure together: South Africa.

Deron had never been, and he longed to see the place I had come from. I was excited at the thought of going back to the place I called home—to show Deron my mango tree, and for him to meet my family, especially Uncle Nicki and his wife Gabi, of whom he'd only heard stories. But alongside the excitement, anxiety loomed. Revisiting the people and places of my youth meant revisiting ghosts. How would I feel seeing those haunted houses again?

When Deron and I arrived in South Africa, my anxiety lifted. This wasn't the place of my youth. This was somewhere I'd never been before. I noticed the difference first by what I didn't see:

"WHITES ONLY BY ORDER,"

"BEWARE OF NATIVES,"

"NON-EUROPEAN HOSPITAL,"

"BEACH AND SEA WHITES ONLY,"

"NON-WHITE SHOP"

The signs were all gone.

Though South Africa had been my home for fourteen years, I was thirty years old before I could walk my homeland unrestricted. This unfamiliar sense of freedom I felt while revisiting familiar landmarks was both beautiful and strange. I heard childhood rhymes and stones sliding on hopscotch squares in places now populated by Whites and Coloureds. I sat at Granny's kitchen table and listened to her whistling kettle. I savored the fragrant steam before taking a sip of the hot tea, made thick and sweet with heaping teaspoons of condensed milk. I could smile, listening to Uncle Johnny strum his guitar in the background.

I took Deron to my beloved mango tree, and we sat together in the dirt, backs against bark, as I shared stories of my life in this place. I felt again that strange mix of the old and new, as we moved together through my past. I had never imagined that one day I would return to sit above these roots with the love of my life. It was there, under the mango tree with Deron, that I came to understand there were more things in heaven and earth than I had dreamt possible. As a child, so much of Father's philosophy had eluded me. "Gillian," he used to say, "you can keep your head in the sky, but only if you keep your feet on the ground." I had not understood how a person could be in two different places at once. I had spent my life climbing above the fray to where I could look down from a place of safety: the wall behind Granny's, the stump at iFafa, my mango tree. Now, here with Deron, with my feet planted in the present, I could finally look up to the sky.

Having been gone for so long, and coming back to a changed world, I saw Africa with new eyes. I could see, for the first time, the stark contrasts that defined it. It was a land of brilliant sunsets and impenetrable darkness, of bounty and want, a womb and a grave. It had been mother to humanity and a startling array of wildlife, only to succumb to colonialism, the values of Christianity, Apartheid, diamonds, and Imperial dreams.

Africa, certainly, had changed, but I had changed, too. Most of all, with Deron by my side, I felt safe enough to open up to my country and to the memories I'd buried there. Deron and I roamed the countryside together without ever having to justify our presence with our race. We drove hundreds of miles through cities, across highways, dirt roads, savannas, and vast grasslands. Everywhere we went, no matter how remote, we were met with an abundance of life. Even the naturally-occurring fires burning over the grasslands smelled of life. I soaked it all in as we drove down deserted roads, and, in some places, even paved our own.

One of the roads we took was to the Kingdom of Lesotho in the middle of South Africa. Before crossing the border into this landlocked country, we stopped to grab lunch at a local restaurant.

"No, this would not be smart," said the waitress when we told her we were driving ourselves through the Sani Pass and into Lesotho. "See, it's wintertime, and you never know what the conditions will be like until you're up there. The road is very windy and dangerous."

So Deron and I did something I would never have imagined a Coloured girl could do in South Africa: we hired a White man, Pete, to chauffeur us. Not so very long before, I would not have even been allowed in a car with this man, and now I was engaging his services. It was surreal.

We had no idea what to expect when we entered Lesotho; after all, we hadn't planned to go. It was one of many spontaneous adventures we'd added to our journey. What we discovered was a nation of just over two million people but as full of complexities and contradictions as the larger country surrounding it.

Deron and I marveled at the spectacular imagery of the Kingdom of Lesotho. We took in daring mountains, brilliant waterfalls, and villages that seemed to have been frozen in time. We saw a country plagued with so many of the problems associated with poverty: hunger, gender inequality, poor education, child abuse, child labor, violence. On top of these struggles, the HIV/AIDS epidemic had hit the Kingdom. The staggering natural beauty coupled with the desperate afflictions of the people contributed an intensity, a sharpness, to every moment we spent there.

After visiting Lesotho, we returned to South Africa, and there, in the country where my life had begun, Kiara was conceived.

29

BACK IN CALIFORNIA, KIARA RAN IN BAREFOOT innocence. She knew nothing of racism, abuse, or abandonment. She knew nothing of her mother's early struggles. Three years later, Nicki arrived. She had Deron's smile, his playful manner, and his creativity.

Before having children, I had questioned if I could ever be a good mother. When I was pregnant with Kiara, I shared my very real concern with Deron: "What if I'm not able to give her the love she will need?" He laughed. "G, I don't know a single person in this world who has more love to give than you. There are things to worry about in this life, but that is not one of them."

After having Kiara and Nicki, all doubt that I could love them in the way a mother should love her children was erased. Kiara and Nicki were more than all the world's oceans, more than every mango tree that ever grew. They were me, and they were Deron, and I loved them in a way I'd never known was possible.

"What new parenting book are you reading now, G?"

"*Emotionally Intelligent Parenting.* By the way, I just finished *Toilet Training In Less Than A Day,* and I think we should apply the principles with Kiara this weekend."

Deron laughed and shook his head: "You need balance," he joked.

He was probably right, but I had made it through college and therapy by being a consummate student, and why should motherhood be any different? I had read bags of books on raising children and researched more online. I had changed my diet so that the girls had the best start to their lives. Having loved burgers and fries in college, I now drank home-made protein shakes loaded with vegetables, and I breastfed Kiara for the first two years of her life. Kiara would not take a bottle, so when I returned to work after two months of maternity leave, I left each day at noon, drove to her grandparents to breastfeed her, then rushed back to work. Though Kiara was a fussy baby who cried frequently, I had endless patience with her and even more love to give. When she was teething, she refused anything artificial I would try to put in her mouth. Instead, her favorite pacifier was my chin. Her bare gums would suck and bite away at the point of my jawbone. Chin up, face toward the sky, I shrieked with laughter as sweet baby drool ran down my neck.

Our home brimmed with warmth and affection. And books. My girls would never be ashamed to read.

Although they had more books than I ever remembered being in the teeny brick building we had called a library back in Greenwood Park, I was careful not to spoil them with things. Rather, I spoiled them with memories they would be proud to carry with them wherever they went in life. For the first ten years of their life, we had no cable in our home. Weekends they were free to watch a favorite DVD for an hour, but life was to be lived with bare feet on the ground and eyes to the sky. We played together in the sun and the rain. We owned no umbrellas or raincoats. Rain boots, yes; they were fun to wear when splashing in puddles.

In college, Deron and I had found common ground over Jodeci, Boyz II Men, Johnny Gill, Marvin Gaye, Maxwell, and Sublime. We had listened to music in the car, in the shower, in bed, at concerts, while cooking together, and with friends. In parenthood, little changed but the artists. Deron's rap songs took a back seat, and songs like "Baby Beluga" by Raffi, Jack Johnson Sing-A-Longs, and You Are My Friend Personalized Kids Music moved through our home. I wasn't an early riser, but it was impossible to wake in a grumpy mood with Deron and the girls singing at the top of their lungs.

My schooling in South Africa had suggested no real expectations for me besides becoming a wife one day; girls were required to take sewing classes while boys studied things like accounting and woodshop. I'd always longed for horizons that were defined by more than my neat uniform dress and the apron from sewing class, with its detailed embroidery of a rooster and a pretty farmhouse.

Thanks to my hard work in college and the support of my husband, I had risen above the ambitions of my schooling. I was the Director of International Student Services at Santa Clara University, just three miles from our home. And together with Deron, we had founded SHIP AID, a nonprofit that shipped thousands of pounds of medical and educational supplies to the country of Lesotho. Almost daily, I shook my head in disbelief at the position I occupied and the life I led. I took nothing for granted.

Deron and I were children at heart: Deron with his innate playfulness, and me with my excitement for even the mundane. Each evening, I anticipated Deron's return from work as eagerly as Kiara and Nicki. They squealed with delight at the sight of Dad's GMC truck pulling into the driveway, and we all ran out to see him. "There's my girls!" Deron would yell, and he would set his computer bag on the pebbled driveway and scoop us into his arms. I had spent most of my life longing to be held by Mummy or Father, to be told in a familiar voice that everything would be okay, to have the words "I love you" whispered in my ear as their arms enveloped me. Such reassurances never came. Kiara and Nicki knew nothing else.

Wrapped in Deron's arm, with two daughters of my own, my body sang.

Deron had taken on a part-time coaching position at a local high school, Harker Academy. Playing in the NFL, he'd found little joy in the game—it was a cutthroat profession utterly misaligned with his own approach to life. Coaching helped rekindle his passion for football, and he found he had a gift for working with young people. He didn't simply tell his students how to play but demonstrated it himself, doing football drills alongside them and running sprints with them. The boys were strengthened by his energy, passion, and larger than life personality. But our days had become exceptionally busy. Working a full-time job at Cisco and coaching part-time, Deron had his hands full; meanwhile, along with my full-time job, I was almost solely responsible for the girls and the household chores. All of this, in addition to running SHIP AID, left us exhausted. I looked forward to the end of football season when Deron would be home again, and both of us would have more time together.

I have learned that pain is patient.

I thought I knew pain intimately. I thought we had a deal: Pain stings; I suffer. Pain fades; I heal. Childhood wounds which had threatened to undo me had turned to scars—a tougher, more resilient skin, resistant to pain. Since the morning Aunt Alvia woke Thurn, Tania, and me in the house on Barnes Road, we had all walked a jagged road. Stripped of the protection promised at my birth, I walked that road unveiled. Years of torturous steps made out of sheer will had hardened my feet. I had outlived the pain.

But pain is perfectly, utterly patient.

It was the first week of November, and fall lay heavy over California. The days were shorter, the nights longer, and chilly mornings made it harder to get out of bed.

I woke up Friday morning, out of sorts, my head foggy. A haze seemed to have settled around me, and I felt anxious as though my mind were puzzling over a problem it couldn't quite figure out. A month before, I had dreamed of death. In my dream, it was Mummy. So vivid was the dream that a month later, it still haunted me: Mummy's body lying stiff in an empty room. I had woken obviously shaken and recounted the dream to Deron.

"Don't worry. It was just a bad dream. Mumalini is fine," he'd said.

Still, I had rushed to the phone and called Mummy, just to make sure she was in fact alive. She'd answered, much to my relief, and until this morning, I had put the dream out of mind. This morning, as always, Deron was blaring Jack Johnson's *Upside Down* to wake our daughters. Kiara was four, and Nicki was seventeen months, and they were laughing at his singing and silly dance moves. This was Granny's tea kettle, and just as then, I got up and began preparing for the day.

I had been looking forward to this Friday for a long time. Today was the final game of Harker Academy's High School football season, and Deron would be home all weekend for the first time in a couple of months. I moved through my morning routine with an automaticity that should have felt comfortable, so why did I feel so off? I couldn't put my finger on anything more than an ominous uncertainty, but it was as charged with inevitability as the air before a storm.

"I like your sweater, G," Deron said with a smile, as I prepared to leave for work.

"Thank you," I replied flatly. I still felt strange and unsettled.

"Are you okay? You seem so serious this morning."

"I'm fine," I answered. I wasn't, but I knew I should be.

Deron worked from home on Fridays, so I remember he carried both Nicki and Kiara out to the car to wave me off. The girls always looked so tiny in his giant arms.

"We love you, Mom!" Deron and Kiara yelled. I pulled away from the house, but before I got too far, I looked into my rearview mirror for one last look at my three heroes outside our home.

I arrived at the office ten minutes late. The memory of my dream from a month before had gripped me for most of the drive in, so I was glad to have something else to focus on. When my work line rang that morning, it was Deron.

"Hi, G, I'm just checking in on you! How are you doing?"

This was typical Deron: he'd noticed I was off this morning and wanted to make sure I was okay. If he knew someone was in need, he felt compelled to help. I loved this about him.

I answered honestly. "I'm not sure how I'm doing, Deron."

"Is it a headache or a stomachache?"

"Neither. I actually don't have any pain. I just feel really odd today."

"You're probably exhausted," he said. "This has been a really busy couple of months for both of us. Why don't you come home early and rest before the girls get home from school."

Deron spoke gently, but with insistence rather than suggestion. I told him I would leave early, though I had no intention of doing so. There was nothing physically wrong with me, and "feeling off" seemed like a poor excuse to leave work. The truth was, I approached my work in the office the way I had approached every endeavor. If I held back even the least bit of effort, I would be filled with guilt. Deron knew this about me and often reminded me to take breaks, just as he had in college.

An hour later, I received an email from Deron: *Where are you? Leave now. Your health is more important than work. DT.* I smiled. Since he was working from home today, there would be no putting him off. I could expect gentle but regular reminders until he saw me pull into the driveway, so I started packing up my things to go home. Deron still knew me, at least as well as I knew myself.

I watched Deron's final game of the season from the stands with Kiara and Nicki. Nicki was only a year and a half old and too young to appreciate what was happening, but throughout the game, Kiara had yelled, "Go Daddy Go!" The final score that night was a 7-0 victory to Harker Academy over Soledad High. Deron had an incredible impact on the team in the short period of time he coached there. He had taken Harker from a 0-10 record the previous year to 7-2, and he beamed with excitement at Harker's final victory of the season. As soon as the game ended, Deron ran over to her.

"Binklebird!" he called, his arms outstretched.

"Your team won, Daddy!"

"They did great, Binklebird!"

I smiled as I watched him take both girls in his arms. He held them with a post-game joy I had not seen during all his years of college football and the NFL.

It was past Nicki's bedtime, so I took her home so Kiara could enjoy part of the after-game celebration with her dad. When they returned, I stood at her bedroom door and watched as Deron settled her in for the night. He dressed Kiara in her pink Elmo nightgown and read her a story as she drifted off to sleep. Then he rose quietly, took my hand and walked with me to the kitchen. He was heading back to Harker for a little celebration with the team and coaches. Before he left, we stood in the silence of the kitchen, and I whispered, "I'm really proud of you, Deron. Really proud of what you accomplished with those kids. You are the reason they were so successful this season."

"Thank you, G. You know, this is the first time in my football career I went out a winner in my final game. I've lost every final game since high school." He smiled broadly, "I know what I want to do when I retire."

I pulled him back into my arms, and we lapsed into silence again. I didn't want Deron to go back out.

I wanted him to stay right where he was, in our home, where I had him all to myself. Deron finally broke our embrace.

"You'll probably be in Kiara's room by the time I get home," he said.

I nodded. In an attempt to wean Nicki off nighttime breast-feedings, I had been sleeping on a twin bed in Kiara's room while Deron slept with Nicki in our bed.

"I'll move Nicki out of her crib and into our room when I get home," he said.

"Thank you," I said. "Please hurry home."

"I love you, G. Please get some rest."

I smiled. "I love you, Deron," I said and watched him as he walked out into the night.

30

WAKE THE NEXT MORNING TO THE SOUND OF Nicki's faint cry. Otherwise, the house is silent. I look over to see Kiara still asleep in her bed. Weird. Where's the music? Where is Deron? Nicki cries again from the master bedroom, so I pull myself out of bed and walk down the hallway toward our room. My breasts are sore and swollen with milk, and Nicki is undoubtedly hungry. I step into the bedroom, and Nicki is sitting in our California king-sized bed—alone.

I am surprised to see her alone. Deron has never left her unattended on the bed before. Further, he promised the girls he would spend the day with them, and he is never one to break a promise, especially when it comes to the girls and me.

Perhaps Deron went out for a morning jog. He's an early riser, and the moment his eyes open, he's up and ready to start the day. It's quite common for him to step out quietly for a run, or a game of basketball, or a bike ride before the girls and I wake up. He's joined a lunch-time league at work, and on some Saturdays and every Sunday, he plays "Church of Hoops" with a group of friends. Still, I'm annoyed he didn't bring Nicki into the bed with me, as he usually did before heading out.

I scoop up Nicki, feed her, and go about my morning ritual of helping Kiara dress. Breakfast is fried eggs. It's been an hour, and Deron is still not home. Since waking up, Kiara has asked a ceaseless rotation of questions: "Where's Dad? When is he coming home? He said he'd take us out today. Where is he?"

I know Deron came back last night because I had been able to sleep. If I go to bed while he's still out, I can't relax until he returns. When I heard the creaking of the front door around midnight, I knew he was home: my cue to fall asleep.

Once asleep, I can sleep through anything.

Kiara finishes eating, and I begin cleaning up. It's ten a.m., and Deron is still not home. Something is not right. I try to brush it off, but the knot that's been form-ing in my stomach since I saw Nicki sitting up in our bed, alone, has swelled into a storm of anxiety. To quiet my anxiety, and Kiara who has not stopped asking about Daddy, I plunk her and Nicki in front of a Barney DVD:

Oh, mister sun, sun, mister golden sun, please
shine down on me
Oh, mister sun, sun, mister golden sun, hiding
behind a tree
These little children are asking you
To please come out so we can play with you

Kiara quiets, placated by the screen, and I reach for the home phone on the kitchen counter to call Deron. That's when I notice his cell phone is charging on the countertop, just where he leaves it before bed. My eyes shift quickly to the garden window. His car sits idle in the driveway. So he didn't drive anywhere. Maybe he biked?

I run to the garage. His bike is there. My anxiety turns to panic.

I run back into the house. Deron's phone is still there. Of course it is. Kiara and Nicki are still in the living room, singing along with Barney. That's something, at least. I pick up a plate. Might as well load the dishwasher. Wait. If his phone, his car, and his bike are still here, then maybe Deron never left the house this morning. I drop the plate I'm holding and run to the master bathroom— the only room I haven't been in that morning.

Deron is there.

His torso is draped sideways over the toilet. His neck is bent, and his forehead is pressed against the glass door of the shower. His legs are stretched as far as the bathroom counter. I've never seen death up close, but I know, with absolute certainty, he is not alive. I feel eyes on me. I wrench my gaze from Deron's stiff body to look up to the bathroom door. It's Kiara. Her frightened face, framed in golden curls, peeks from behind the door. Suddenly, I cannot breathe. I cannot see. The room spins. My legs fail, and I fall to the floor beside Deron.

MEMORIES OF THAT DAY LIVE AS FLEETING moments in time, disconnected from a larger narrative: Deron's body lying on the bathroom floor, helpless. Tears. Fire trucks. An ambulance. Screaming. Crying. Strangers in our home. Barney. Nicki dancing. Mummy vomiting in the back yard. My hands shaking, unable to hold the phone. Deron's parents. Tania's voice: *You're joking, right?*

Once again, death has crept into my home with a grab and a snatch. Where there were five, only four remained. Where there had been four, there are now only three.

I kicked a kitchen cabinet the day he left. It was a kick directed at God. *How the hell could you have given me something so beautiful only to snatch it away?* All I got back was a swollen right foot. Pain became my new skin.

I AM LYING ON A COUCH IN MY IN-LAWS' LIVING room, begging, pleading, crying until even tears fail me.

A voice from the kitchen: "What's her medical number?"

Another voice: "Gillian, focus. What's your medical record number?" It's Tania.

"I don't know."

"Who is your doctor?"

"I don't know."

Nothing matters. The tears start again.

Another voice: "We have to get her something to calm her down."

The rationale of this assertion eludes me. *Calm me down? Deron is dead! Why in the hell should anyone be calm?*

Medication is delivered and administered. It is like waking from a nightmare to find my arms and legs tangled in the sheets, and I can't get free. I move in a medicated haze through everyone else's world, imprisoned and unable to feel. I live and relive Deron's death over and over and over again.

His clothes still hang in the closet, with his size 16 shoes neatly lined up below.

Some days, I dial his cell phone, hoping he will answer, but he never does. Every time I call I get the same recording: "The number you have dialed is no longer in service. If you feel that you have reached this number in error, please hang up and dial again." And I do. I dial again, and again.

I exist only for Kiara and Nicki. There will be no boarding school to play surrogate parent. No man to rescue me. No alcohol to drown out the only two emotions I feel anymore: agonizing pain and apathy.

Kiara and Nicki no longer sleep in their rooms. They join me in the California king Deron and I had once shared. It is comfort each of us desperately needs. On one side lies Nicki, her head tucked under my arm and her little hands clinging to my abdomen. On the other side lies Kiara, her tears wetting my shoulder. As painful as it is to hear her cries, I do not silence her as I had been. She will always have my shoulder to cry on: "When you miss someone you love, it is okay to be sad. Cry and let the pain out. It's okay."

ONE MIGHT SUGGEST MY DAUGHTERS SAVED MY life.

Did they? Perhaps. One can never know what might have been. But this I know: during the months of emptiness and sterility following Deron's death, the only reason I ever had to wake up in the morning was Kiara and Nicki. The only reason I ever had to play music again was them.

The three of us felt Deron's absence everywhere. Kiara and I attended weekly grief counseling sessions. When Nicki got older, she joined us. Even at seventeen months, Nicki grappled with the incomprehensible sadness of loss. Sleeping in the back of the car one day, she abruptly woke with her hands stretched out and yelled, "Dadda!" Startled, I looked back at her through the rearview mirror. She was smiling. Then she must have realized Deron wasn't there, and the smile disappeared. A few days later, she saw a tall man with blond hair run past, and she called after him, "Dadda, Dadda!" Watching her little disappointments, again and again, was enough to break me all over again.

Kiara, at four years old, was just a few months older than I had been when my father died, and she ached with all her soul. Like me at her age, Kiara had paid attention to more than one might think. She remembered her dad's arms, the feel of his hair in her hands, and his smile, every bit as much as I did. With her near-photographic memory, she remembers other things I would like her to forget. She remembers finding his body with me. She remembers me collapsing, as though the earth beneath my feet had shifted suddenly. She couldn't contextualize what was happening, the way an adult might. She began to wonder if her grandparents or I would be lost—just gone one day, without warning. A fear took root in her that wouldn't be exorcised for many years. I ached to think of Deron seeing her in such distress; he had always been the protector, the partner. He could ease with a smile, but now it was my turn to smile. I had to. When I could, I hummed a familiar tune:

"Smile, when your heart is breaking,
  smile, even though it's aching . . ."

THREE MONTHS AFTER DERON'S DEATH, I RECEIVED a death certificate that read: CARDIAC ARRHYTHMIA— NATURAL. We collectively shook our heads. I say we because although I had lost a husband, Deron's parents had lost a son. It was 2006. We were living in a time where scientific and medical advances had been growing exponentially over centuries. Highly skilled doctors who had trained and practiced for years were charged with identifying the cause of death. They took apart my husband. Every organ they examined was healthy. Every cell they inspected was normal. Anything that might have been wrong was not, so with nothing to point to, they pointed to Deron's heart. Though the heart was not enlarged and though it appeared to be healthy, the final determination of these highly skilled doctors was that a "natural" cardiac arrhythmia was to blame. At the age of thirty-three, Deron had been taken by quiet, apathetic, heartless death, and science wrapped up their investigation with a helpless shrug, a callous "Meh."

I wanted answers. Someone out there must have the answer, I thought, if I only knew where to look. I went online, but I didn't even know what words to type into the search bar.

A friend of Deron's put forward his theory: "I think we have a finite amount of heartbeats and Deron used up his in thirty-three years. I mean, I don't know anybody who lived a fuller life than him."

I appreciated his sentiment, but this was a load of crap. Child molesters and rapists lived to ninety. Babies caught the flu and died before their first birthday. Something had killed my husband, and it wasn't lightning, a snakebite, or bad food. I became tired of the downward glances, the dithering, the hemming and hawing, and a death certificate telling me only what didn't kill him.

With the death certificate in front of me, I could no longer pretend. I finally placed the order for Deron's gravestone.

31

EARLY ON IN OUR MARRIAGE, DERON AND I HAD a brief conversation about death.

"There really is no need for an expensive burial," he had said. "I won't know the difference. Save the money and use it for something else." I agreed. Why wouldn't I? Death was a mere abstraction at the time; Deron and I had years of life ahead of us.

We had decided we would be cremated.

Now that Deron was actually dead, the idea I would have his body cremated because it was the least expensive option allowing me money I could use for something else was absurd in the extreme. I didn't want anything else. I wanted Deron, and I certainly didn't want to have his body burned. Even if it was just an empty shell, I needed to know that he was still somewhere, comfortable, and in a form I was familiar with.

I chose an expensive padded casket that was the exact opposite of anything I could imagine him wanting. He'd have scoffed at the mahogany finish, buffed to a high-gloss, the silver accents, and the white crepe padding. "G!" he would have said, "Are you crazy? I don't need all this. I mean, if you have to put me in a box, give me the simplest wooden box you can find." I knew this, but I got him the casket anyway.

The day before his funeral, there was a wake. Kiara and Nicki were both in attendance. It was important to me that they got to say their final goodbyes. I didn't want them to wonder, as I had, whether their father would ever be returning home. They needed to know that he was gone.

Deron lay in the elaborate casket I'd gotten for him, an artificial smile frozen on his face, put there by whoever did his makeup. His usually rosy pink cheeks were ash-colored. Scott, his roommate from UNR, joked, "Man, Deron would punch whoever put this shit on his face. Big D doesn't wear no makeup. Come on, man! What the hell is this shit all about?"

Kiara had written him a note: *I hope the sun always shines on you Daddy. I love you.* She walked with me to the casket and placed her letter on his folded arms, and watched as I bent over and gently kissed his hard, cold lips for the last time. There would be no more warm hugs, no goofy "I know you like me." No, "It's going to be okay, G." Which was just as well, because I knew it would never be okay.

At Deron's funeral the next day, they called him a mentor, a friend, a "gentle giant." They talked about how he had inspired their children and others. His supervisor at Cisco Systems read a funny email Deron had written. One friend described a plan to plant a birch grove in Deron's honor so that one day "I can sit under the great shade and shelter of Deron's friendship—and keep my eye on him, 'cause he's a bit unruly at times." One by one, the people in Deron's life shared what he meant to them, how he'd made their worlds better.

I heard the words, but I remained unmoved. I hid my tears, allowing them to fall only at nighttime when no one was watching. And when no one was watching, I turned to Deron in impotent anger: *How could you leave? You promised me! You promised things would be different—life would be different. That you would never leave. But then you left, too.*

Our last night out together had been a 49ers fundraising gala. We'd been like college students again, playfully raising our auction sticks, laughing all the way home. I could still hear us, smell the Irish Spring soap on his skin, taste the red wine we'd sipped together. I held onto everything from that night that reminded me of him. Six months after his death, the nail polish was still on my toes. The memories would keep him alive, I thought, and if he were alive, I would feel happy. But death had left the memories hollow and stripped of joy; they did nothing but remind me he was gone.

Sitting in our Santa Clara home, Kiara flipped through the book of letters from Deron's high school football team, where they shared their memories of him. What she loved most were the pictures of her father on the football field. He always looked so happy there.

"Mama," Kiara said. "When I saw Daddy on the floor, I wanted to hug him, but I was scared because I know people don't sleep in the bathroom."

"I know, darling," I said. "Don't you worry. You gave him all the hugs he could have ever wanted."

My father was left in Kimberly to be raised by his grandmother while his mother moved to Cape Town with her new husband. He would not see his mother again until he was a teenager. My mother was raised by an abusive man who watched his youngest daughter step into the street and be hit by a car. She would be left by her husband, the only man who might have shown her how to give and receive love.

I am my mother's daughter. I am my father's daughter. Abandoned. Cracked. Recracked. Shattered. Rebuilt. Kiara and Nicki will have a different mother than either of my parents had.

For six years after Deron died, Kiara clung to my side. She wouldn't use a bathroom unless I stood right by her. She wouldn't let me use the bathroom or take a shower unless she could watch over me. When I dropped her off at school, her peers looked on as she screamed and pleaded with me not to leave her. She would have regular conversations with Deron on the phone. Holding her play-phone to her ear one day, she said, "Hi Dad, I went to school today, and I missed you. When are you coming home?"

IT IS EARLY EVENING. FOR DINNER, I HAVE PRE-pared a garlic-crusted rack of lamb, roasted potatoes, and a strawberry arugula salad. Sitting at our large granite countertop in the middle of our kitchen, Kiara rips her teeth into a lamb chop. With a mouth full of meat and with balsamic salad dressing dripping down her chin, she asks, "Mom, what is God?"

Before I can respond, Nicki says, "God is a fairy, and She is a girl."

Her mouth is still full, but Kiara laughs. I smile and say, "Who's to say Nicki isn't correct?"

32

IMAGINE YOU ARE HOVERING THOUSANDS OF FEET above the West Coast of the United States, where the sky is tinged with the darkness of space. Dive into the sea of clouds stretching below you, drawing closer and closer to the surface of the Earth until you've broken through the clouds to where the North American continent and the largest ocean in the world meet: the Pacific coast. If you are 2,580 miles north of the equator and if you keep your eye trained on the coast, it will be drawn to a gap in the coastline, which opens into San Francisco Bay. Follow the western edge of the bay south, meandering over the peninsula to see the greatest accumulation of wealth in the entire world in towns like Palo Alto, Mountain View, and Atherton, although at this height, borders are indistinguishable and the land will appear as nothing more than a collection of buildings and roads stretching for miles. Let your eye continue to drift south until it settles on Santa Clara—a city of some 130,000 people situated fifty miles south of San Francisco between the Guadalupe River to the east and Saratoga Creek to the west. Look closer, and you will find pleasant strips of restaurants and cafés, well-kept parks, busy highways, and wide streets. Follow one of Santa Clara's wide thoroughfares through a spread of neighborhoods of single-family ranch homes built in the 1960s and 1970s, and look for a back yard where a majestic tree anchors a rope swing on one side and a zipline on the other.

Follow the sturdy trunk to the ground, and you will see the figure of a woman in her forties leaning against the bark; her face is framed by wild kinky curls. Her legs are outstretched on the grass, and her feet are bare. Next to her in the grass are a pair of Skechers tennis shoes. Thirty years ago, this woman most certainly would have found Santa Clara's streets and shops and suburban sprawl humdrum. Now it is home.

It has been twelve years since Deron's passing. There's a new president, new world struggles, news from my family in South Africa. Kiara and Nicki are teenagers now and no longer subject to the fear and uncertainty that haunted them over a decade ago. My American-born daughters view freedom as their birthright, and though the paths they choose to walk may not be the ones I would have chosen for them, I am grateful they've never questioned their right to make those choices.

When Kiara was growing in my belly, I thought I had it all figured out. I would raise a strong female whose self-worth would not be defined by society's standards of how a girl should behave and look. I introduced her to planes, Africa, the outdoors; I painted her bedroom lemon yellow with a sky-blue ceiling and neon stars that would take her imagination out of the confines of billboards and television. But in her freedom, she chose to reject space, planes, trains, the color blue, the color yellow. She loves pink and all things sparkling. At five years old, when a modeling scout approached us in the mall, she pleaded with me to let her model.

"Sweetie," I told her, "you're too young for such a business."

"No, I'm not, Mom! Please, please, pleeease let me be a model."

This pleading went on for some time until I finally conceded that if she still wanted to be a model when she turned thirteen, I would support it. With a stubbornness I must admit felt quite familiar, she reminded me of that promise two days before her thirteenth birthday. Though I still felt hesitant, Nicki, my little sage, chimed in: "Mom, let Kiara be her own person."

Nicki is a sentimental, sensitive type, often introverted, but can also burst forth in fits of energy and profound wisdom. She was a baby when Deron died, so he is a myth to her. She is always asking Kiara and me to share stories of her dad so that our memories of him will become hers. She looks intensely at photos of a man she never knew, scouring them for clues, pondering conversations they never had. She's not overly sad about it, but it's a chasm she will never cross. She tries to build a bridge across the divide, adding bits of color and flesh to the story wherever she can.

Though Nicki doesn't remember Deron, she is the most like him. She has a business mind, just like her father, and a savvy intuition to match his education. Like him, she's highly practical—but also not afraid to take chances. Every week she comes up with a new idea to make money, to start a business, or improve on something that seems inefficient. She's made tidy profits in event planning, dumpster diving, dog sitting, and more. Once, as I sat in the kitchen helping with her latest venture, Nicki turned to me and said, "Mom, I hope one day we can have a business together because working with you is really fun."

SEVEN YEARS AFTER DERON DIED, WHEN KIARA WAS eleven and Nicki eight, I attended a speaker series called "The Search for What Matters." As one guest speaker, a former faculty member at Santa Clara University, talked about her decision to resign from the university and spend the year afterward gardening and weeding, I listened with growing frustration. I bristled at her arrogance and at the presumptuous privilege. She had a husband who supported her decision and paid the bills while she sorted things out in her life. I didn't have anyone to pick up the slack for me while I did the same, and I was sure I wasn't the only one in the audience with my challenges. I left the series annoyed, but for weeks after, I thought about her talk. It was true I did not have the luxuries she did, but it was also true that I was searching for excuses.

Living with Marcel had been like swimming in a storm, stealing breaths, fighting to stay above water, living on the edge of drowning. I'd spent the last two decades enjoying the freedom of having my feet on stable shores. My bouts with PTSD had thrown me back into the water, but I'd had Deron to keep me afloat and bring me back to shore. With his death, I had felt the pull of those deep waters again, but Kiara and Nicki had kept me moored. I wanted to spend more time with them, to watch and support and shape them during their formative years: the years I had spent so alone and scared. I wanted the flexibility to pick them up from school, to spend time with them in the afternoons, to make dinners that were not rushed. I wanted to spend the unhurried hours with them, hours I hadn't had with my father and had always wanted with my mother. I had spent my life escaping various shackles on my freedom, and I realized my job had become another one. I understood the man in Mark Nepo's *The Book of Awakening,* left at sea on a burning boat with two choices: stay and surely die or jump and possibly live. Staying at my job meant leaving Kiara and Nicki with their grandparents after school while I spent all day away from them. Having suffered prolonged absences from my mother following my own father's death, and being aware of the girls' connection with Deron, I wanted to avoid any anxiety they might have about any absences of mine. I would choose another path, and I would have to do it alone. But, I had learned I could do that.

When I made the decision to leave the university, I jumped into the sea, not knowing what lurked in the waters below.

First, I embarked on a business venture that failed miserably. I lost a good chunk of my savings but learned some valuable life lessons in the process: know your business partner as well as you would a significant other before saying "I do;" trust your gut; and never be afraid to walk away. When I finally did, I went back to the field of education, but this time as an independent educational consultant. This role has no shackles. It grants me the flexibility to be present with Kiara and Nicki while still helping others.

There are sharks and rough waters at times, but I forge ahead. Occasionally I drift in winds and waves more powerful than me, but this doesn't frighten me as it once did. I am protected by the universe, which rewards my choices as it always has, granting me power for pain. My strokes are not always clean or as powerful as I would like, but as long as my compass is true, I will never breach dangerous shoals or shores.

My past is set in stone. My present, however, is fluid, and each breath I take is mine and mine alone.

I have gained so much.

What are the odds a Coloured girl once stranded on a remote farm in Africa would have made it here? I was never expected to attend college, yet I have two degrees. I knew little of love or intimacy, yet I now give and receive love in abundance. Where I thought I had lost a star, I have received constellations, and Deron, my star, still rises.

He rises out of a broken pot that lays in the garden. It is one of three Spanish clay pots he gave me. Its many breaks have been crudely mended. A geranium stem has worked its way out of a crack, and in its blossoms, I'm reminded of the beauty in imperfections. Unlike the other two pots, neatly perched on a fence that borders the garden, the cracked one suggests a richer life holding lessons and treasures the others lack. Deron rises out of a ladder he assembled many years back as part of a bunk bed for the girls. The girls have grown out of the bed, but the ladder leans lopsidedly against the tree where their little feet once climbed.

The tree is a giant. I bought the house because of that tree, remembering the tall, sturdy mango tree that had given me refuge and sweetness during my youth. I hoped my girls would never need to find safety in a tree, but it gave me comfort to know it was there watching over them just as my tree in Durban had watched over me.

I have no certainty of what tomorrow holds, but I harbor no fear. Something firmly rooted cannot be stolen. From the day my father walked out of our house that final evening, through the deaths and depression, the loss and the love, the oppression and openness, the confusion and clarity, my roots have grown. I am anchored by Deron—as sturdy and big in memory as he was in life. I am anchored by our girls, who remind me that agency is a birthright. I am anchored by my African ancestors, who taught me it's easier to breathe when you walk rather than when you run. I am anchored by my choices, that remind me I am not defined by my past.

I have sat in the back seat of so many cars in my life, which took me to places I would never have chosen to go: iFafa, Marcel's house, California, Nevada. Each time the uncertainty of where I was going and why I was being taken there filled me with dread. Today, back against the tree, bare feet in the grass, I have left the back seat for a place in the front with a full view of my present. I don't always know my destination, but instead of dread, I am filled with wonder.

There is a saying, "Whom the Gods would destroy, they first make proud." The inverse corollary of this is: "Whom the Gods would elevate, they first must humble."

I have indeed been humbled, beginning with a theft occurring only moments after my birth. I wonder how different my life would have been if I had walked around with that piece of dried skin, relying on it to protect me.

The sun has set. I can hear the girls laughing from inside the house, and I smile into the warm California evening. I dare the thieves to come, to test me once more. When they come, I will not clamber up the branches of another tree and hide. I am done hiding.

The Santa Clara breeze moves softly through the branches above me. I stand and scoop up my Skechers. Kiara and Nicki desperately wish I would wear something more trendy, like Adidas. They hide my shoes, hoping it will incentivize me to buy a new pair. But they are wrong. Where my girls were born with a sense of utter belonging—in their bodies, their clothing, their dreams, their personalities—I have, after many years, constructed a world in which I belong. My beat-up Ske-chers, and the loving scorn accompanying them, are part of that world.

I walk toward the house. Lights blaze through the windows and pitch the ground beneath me into dark-ness. My legs are sore from sitting, but the steps I take are strong. Kiara and Nicki's voices drift from the house and dance with the rustling leaves of the tree behind me. One of them says, "I don't even know if I'm really related to you!" and the other one laughs and says, "You know you like me."

I glance at our driveway, at the spacious car that fer-ries us easily wherever we need to go; it dwarfs the majes-tic red Fiat of my youth. Behind me, my giant American tree breathes gently in the blackness. For some reason, I think of Granny and her bush knife, and I smile. Then I open the door of our Santa Clara home and step inside.

Dedication and Acknowledgments

THIS BOOK IS FIRST AND FOREMOST DEDICATED to my late husband, Deron Thorp, the most loving and tender human being I've ever known. A long time ago Deron suggested I write about my life. My usual response was, "sure, maybe someday." Although that *someday* has finally arrived, the story has changed in ways I could never have imagined. Before, it was the story of me. Now, at the heart of the story is us. I miss you so, my darling. Thank you for always believing in me.

I also want to thank our daughters Kiara and Nicki. Your strength and resilience make me believe I can move boulders (even big ones). Thank you, my suns, for your love and patience in putting up with me throughout the process of writing this book. For understanding its importance to me and encouraging me. I am deeply honored to call you my daughters.

To Granny, a true African Warrior whose sacrifices shall never be forgotten. Thank you for teaching me the meaning of courage.

Thank you, Jay Christopher, the best editor any writer could ask for. As Stephen King once wrote, "to write is human, to edit divine." You are indeed the "divine" in this equation. Your careful eye and attention to detail was masterful. I am beyond grateful for your commitment to this tale.

A big shout-out to Shauna for your careful reading and rereading. Your thoughtful and beautiful feedback made this book all the more better.

Thank you, Lisa Kusel. I knocked on your author door (virtually) and you didn't for a moment hesitate to let me in. As if reading my book and offering invaluable feedback wasn't enough, you also generously offered to take my hand and coach me through the confusing and (sometimes crazy) world of publishing. You are a rare treasure and an amazing writer.

To Frank, for all of your encouragement and devoted support over the years. Thank you for listening when I needed a pair of ears. Then listening again and again. Your friendship is a gift.

To all my many family and friends who contributed to the creation and completion of this book (from filling in the gaps to cover design input and everything in between)—a heartfelt thank you.

About the Author

GILLIAN THORP LIVES BETWEEN HOMES IN THE San Francisco Bay Area and east of the Sierra Nevada. She has two daughters, Kiara and Nicki. Born Gillian August, she earned a Bachelor of Science in Psychology from the University of Nevada, Reno and a Master of Arts in Counseling from Santa Clara University. Her educational background has given her a deep understanding of the human psyche and a broad base from which to approach many topics.

In 2001, Gillian began working at Santa Clara University as Director, International Students and Scholars and served in this role for over a decade. She remains affiliated with the university as a member of the Undergraduate Admissions Committee, selecting candidates for admission. Gillian has written many college papers, business plans, departmental newsletters, and copious student materials.

Over the years, Gillian has journaled extensively with personal writings but her more serious writing did not develop until after her husband, NFL player, Deron Thorp unexpectedly passed away in 2006. Writing a book has been on her bucket list for many years, and eventually with The Colour of the Sun, it became a reality.

When Gillian is not reading, writing, gardening, singing badly to music she loves and raising her daughters to be women, she can be found volunteering and helping others in need. Find out more about Gillian at gillianthorp.com

Advance Praise for
Gillian Thorp's *The Colour of the Sun*

"Avid readers know there are some stories that don't just stick with you; they become a part of you. They live deep within the crevices of your mind and completely reshape the lens with which you view the world. This is one of those stories. In *The Colour of the Sun*, Thorp unabashedly shares her own gripping life story to shed light upon the parts of humanity that haunt most of us like a shadow— racism, mental illness, abuse, addiction, violence, loneliness. And yet, a story punctuated by such a devastatingly steady stream of misfortune is threaded by perseverance, by strength, by education, and—most importantly—by love. In one single book, Thorp manages to encapsulate the entirety of what it is to be human."

—Candice Jalili, author of *Just Send the Text*

"Thorp isn't being modest when she says, 'I have always been a keen observer with a memory for the minutiae of a moment. . . .' *The Colour of the Sun* brims with gritty sensual details. Whether she is recounting her peripatetic and turbulent childhood in South Africa, the social isolation she experiences as an illegal immigrant in America, or the agony of depression just when she finally finds her footing, Thorp holds nothing back, and for that, I was indelibly grateful. A terrific compelling read."

—Lisa Kusel, author of *Rash*

"Gillian Thorp's story of a childhood in South Africa, an adolescence in California, and an adulthood marked by profound grief and resilience is a gripping read. Racism,

abuse, loss seem to follow her wherever she goes, until she builds the courage to stand up to them and for herself and her children. This book combines the grit and determinism of Cheryl Strayed's *Wild* with the vivid realism of Alexandra Fuller's *Don't Let's Go to the Dogs Tonight.*"
—Jan Johnson, publisher emerita Red Wheel/Weiser Books and independent publishing consultant

"From the very first line of 'I was born among thieves,' I was hooked. *The Colour of the Sun* is an incredible, honest journey through the extraordinary life of Gillian Thorp. Thorp delivers an emotional memoir with a touch of humor from the figures in her life, to the challenges of growing up under Apartheid South Africa to the struggles of coming to America and starting a family. Thorp is a wonderful storyteller who takes the reader on a rollercoaster ride through a mixture of extreme heartbreak to pure joy. Once I started, I could not put it down. *The Colour of the Sun* is a terrific memoir."
—Scott Magruder, Digital Content Producer, News 4 & Fox 11

CPSIA information can be obtained
at www.ICGtesting.com
Printed in the USA
LVHW030707241220
674973LV00003B/384